# WORKING LEGS

| MISTER BLAND | THE MANAGER | SOCIAL WORKER |
|---|---|---|

| BETTY MACRAE | ABLE McMANN | MISS SHY |
|---|---|---|

| THAT ALEX | MEG OF SUPPLY | OUR EDITOR |
|---|---|---|

# WORKING LEGS

A Two-Act Play For
Disabled Performers
by
Alasdair Gray

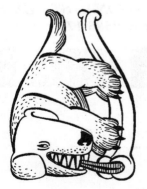

DOG AND BONE
GLASGOW 1997

*THIS PLAYBOOK WAS FIRST PUBLISHED
IN 1997 BY DOG & BONE PRESS,
2 MARCHMONT TERRACE,
GLASGOW G12 9LT*

*SCENES 8 AND 9 WERE PRINTED IN WEST
COAST MAGAZINE ISSUE 23 IN 1996,
SCENES 2 AND 10 IN THE GLASGOW
HERALD, 15 NOVEMBER 1997*

*DESIGNED BY ALASDAIR GRAY,
TYPESET BY EM-DEE PRODUCTIONS,
389 PAISLEY ROAD WEST,GLASGOW G51 1LR*

*PRINTED AND BOUND BY BELL & BAIN
303 BURNFIELD ROAD, THORNLIEBANK,
GLASGOW G46 7UQ*

*GLASGOW CITY & SCOTTISH ARTS COUNCILS
GAVE MONEY TO PUBLISH THIS BOOK*

*THE INTERNATIONAL STANDARD BOOK
NUMBER IS 1-872536-17-4*

*TO BARONESS THATCHER AND ALL THE
RIGHT HONOURABLE
HUMPTY DIPSIES
WHO HAVE MADE
OUR NEW,
LEAN, FIT,
EFFICIENT
BRITAIN.*

# CAST AND

Unless stated otherwise below all actors perform in wheelchairs. Where sex not given, actors can be either.

ABLE McMANN, a youngish man with working legs and, usually, a wheelchair. He in ALL SCENES BUT 10 AND 11

| | |
|---|---|
| BARTENDER: | SCENES 1, 9 |
| THRUST, a business person: | SCENES 1, 9 |
| BLAND, a big businessman: | SCENES 1, 7, 9 |
| COY, a seductive woman: | SCENES 1, 9 |
| SUAVE, a seductive man: | SCENES 1, 9 |
| SOCIAL WORKER, blind: | SCENES 1, 5, 12 |
| MANAGER, a business person: | SCENES 2, 3, 5, 12 |
| BETTY MACRAE, our heroine: | SCENES 3, 4, 6, 12 |

UNDERMANAGER, WAITRESS, BETH, LIZ, ALEX, SANDY, LEX: All but waitress wear party paper hats. Alex wears a flamboyant waistcoat. Liz and Lex are not essential.                                    SCENE 3

| | |
|---|---|
| MRS MACRAE, Betty's mother: | SCENES 4, 6, 12 |
| MR MACRAE, Betty's father: | SCENES 4, 6, 12 |

PRIME MINISTER, blind:                    SCENE 5

MEG, a conscientious office worker:        SCENE 6

FOUR DEAF MUTES constituting a benefit tribunal, and APPLICANT with working legs and one line.    SCENE 7

MISS SHY, who has working legs:        SCENES 9, 10, 12

FOUR POLICEMEN: no lines, at the end of        SCENE 9

REPORTER and SUB-EDITOR                SCENE 10

EDITOR:                                SCENES 10, 12

NURSE, SISTER, ANAESTHETIST, HOUSE–OFFICER, SURGEON, ADMINISTRATOR.    SCENE 11

HOSPITAL DOCTOR:                        SCENE 12

POLITICIAN and JUDGE,  ALTERNATIVE SCENE 11

# CONTENTS

As in Shakespeare's theatre scenes can be set by properties.
These, except 9 essential wheelchairs, are listed below.

# ACT ONE: BACK TO NORMAL

# ACT TWO: ROAD TO RUIN

## ACT ONE
## BACK TO NORMAL

John Campbell
as Able McMann
5 October 1997

# SCENE 1 : LOUNGE BAR

CAST : ABLE, BARTENDER, THRUST, BLAND,
COY, SUAVE and SOCIAL WORKER.

*Beside a low gantry of bottles and glasses* BARTENDER
*sits slowly drying a glass and listening to the
conversations of seated customers.* ABLE *stands
awkwardly nearby. He wears jeans, a sweater, a small
knapsack and is trying and failing to catch attention
without shouting.* THRUST *and* BLAND *discuss business,*
COY *and* SUAVE *are obviously flirting. Both couples
have nearly empty glasses on their chair armrests.*

THRUST

He comes from the shoot 'em kill 'em brigade into
contract management and doesn't even know that
a contract locks you into a fixed profit margin.

BLAND
[*nods and smiles*]
So he was no use to you.

THRUST
None at all. Same again?

BLAND
Why not?

THRUST
[*loudly, to* BARTENDER]
Same again please!

BARTENDER
Certainly sir.
[BARTENDER *pours two gins and tonics.*]

COY
[*slyly*]
I told her Bill McGuffie and I had a passionate love affair last year. She said, "But Bill's a married man!" I said, "A year ago I was a married woman!"

[SUAVE *chuckles and pats her hand*]

COY
I wish you'd seen her face!

SUAVE
So do I! Shall we be wicked and have another?

[COY *nods.*]

SUAVE
[*loudly*]
Same again please!

BARTENDER
In a minute sir!

[Bartender *takes liquor to* THRUST *and* BLAND.]

SUAVE
[*intimately, to* COY]
You've a wild sense of humour. I could never fall for a woman who didn't have a wild sense of humour.

[COY *simpers.*]

THRUST
There are two levels to everything. If your profit margin looks significant on your reading of the top

twenty then you may have a level one situation.

[BARTENDER *places glasses on* THRUST *and* BLAND's
*armrests.*]


### BLAND

Or you may have a dinosaur. Nowadays all big killings are made in property. I'd go into property myself if I was five years younger. My turn to pay.

[BLAND *puts money on the* BARTENDER's *armrest.*]


### BARTENDER
Thank you sir.
[*to* SUAVE *while returning to gantry*]
Two gins and tonics was it sir?


### SUAVE
That's right.


### ABLE
[*desperately*]
Listen, I've been waiting for fifteen minutes and you're still serving people who came in after me!

[*General embarrassment. Company look at each other,* THRUST *grinning,* BLAND *shrugging.* SUAVE *taps the side of his head with a finger,* COY *sighs and adopts an appearance of patient waiting.*]


### BARTENDER
[*stiffly*]
I'm not unsympathetic sir, but it's not easy to notice people whose heads aren't at the usual level. What exactly do you want?

ABLE
[*defiantly*]
A large whisky.


BARTENDER
A large whisky?


ABLE
Yes!


BARTENDER
Are you sure that won't have a bad effect on your condition?


ABLE
What has my condition to do with what I drink?


BARTENDER
[*offended but trying not to show it*]
I'm not unsympathetic sir but spirits can harm people in your condition. We had one here last year who went berserk – kicked out all round – knocked four policemen out of their chairs before they dragged him out.


ABLE
[*violently*]
I'm not the violent sort!


BARTENDER
Better safe than sorry. I'll get you a soda water and lime.


ABLE
[*almost yelling*]
Now listen!

[*General tension. Enter blind* SOCIAL WORKER, *swiftly.*]   5

*LOUNGE*
*BAR*

### SOCIAL WORKER
[*loudly and cheerfully*]
I know that voice! It's all right – I can vouch for him
– he's a friend of mine.

[*All but* ABLE *relax.*]

### SOCIAL WORKER
[*to* ABLE]
Calm down. Where's the barstaff?

### BARTENDER
Here sir.

### SOCIAL WORKER
I'm his social worker. Give him a drink.

### BARTENDER
What does he want?

### SOCIAL WORKER
[*to* ABLE]
What do you want?

### ABLE
Whisky.

### SOCIAL WORKER
[*to* BARTENDER]
A small glass for him, large G and T for me. [*to* ABLE]
Sit down! It's hard to hear you at that altitude.

[BARTENDER *goes to gantry.* ABLE *removes his knapsack
and takes out a small folding stool.*]

ABLE
People shouldn't treat me like that.

SOCIAL WORKER
I know you're as sensible as the rest of us but look
at it another way. A lot of unempowered folk turn
bitter and aggressive. No wonder!

[ABLE *squats on the stool.* THRUST, *BLAND,* COY *and* SUAVE
*react approvingly and prepare to enjoy their drinks.*]

SOCIAL WORKER
I've news for you.

ABLE
Yes?

SOCIAL WORKER
A job interview. Tomorrow.

ABLE
[*jumping to his feet*]
A job!

[*Everyone reacts nervously. The* BARTENDER *spills a
whisky then grimly reaches for a soda water.*]

SOCIAL WORKER
[*scowling*]
I told you to calm down and sit!

[*With effort* ABLE *sits. Widespread relief.*]

ABLE
I'm sorry. It hardly ever happens but whenever I

hear a bit of good news I seem to need to jump up
and walk about a bit. After five idle years! A job!

### SOCIAL WORKER

A job *interview*! And you haven't a hope in hell if
you don't learn to control yourself.

### ABLE
What's the firm?

### SOCIAL WORKER

National Equilibrium. It employs hyperactive
people through an arrangement with Social Welfare.
But you won't survive your probation — you won't
survive your interview if you don't cut out these
involuntary movements and keep your temper.

[ABLE *nurses the knapsack on his knee, rocking
backwards and forwards slightly and muttering:*]

### ABLE
I *will* control myself. I will.

### SOCIAL WORKER
Let's drink to that.

### BARTENDER
[*to* SOCIAL WORKER]
Your gin and tonic sir.
[*to* ABLE]
*Here's your soda water and lime.*

### ABLE
[*loudly*]
But . . .

[BARTENDER *faces him defiantly*, SOCIAL WORKER *sternly*, THRUST *annoyed*, BLAND *amused*, COY *worried*. SUAVE *sighs and raises eyes to heaven. After a moment* ABLE *fumbles in his pocket.*]

ABLE
[*quietly*]
Let me pay for this.

[SOCIAL WORKER *smiles and nods approval.*]

# 2 : MANAGER'S OFFICE

CAST : ABLE and COMPANY MANAGER

*A pool of light surrounds a desk with impressive wheelchair behind, less impressive one in front, a telephone and typed letter on top. In shadow to one side is a door four and a half feet high. The MANAGER sits in the larger chair, the smaller is empty. The MANAGER has a kind, polite voice and manner but looks hard at ABLE without smiling or moving her chair throughout the interview.*

MANAGER
[*on telephone*]
I'm ready for him.

[*She lays phone down and sits back waiting. A moment later the door is faintly tapped.*]

MANAGER
Come in!
[ABLE *opens door, enters stooping and squints upward as door shuts behind him.*]

MANAGER
Stand up Mr McMann, we've plenty of headroom.

ABLE
[*standing erect*]
Thank you madam.

MANAGER
[*pointing*]
There's an empty chair. Can you use it?

ABLE
[*coming near*]
Frankly, madam, so much depends on this interview
that I can't help feeling nervous, and when nervous I
prefer to stand.

MANAGER
[*nodding*]
Your problem is psychological.

ABLE
[*hurt*]
No! I get cramp when I don't exercise, the doctors say
that always happens in legs with working muscles.

MANAGER
Your hyperactive legs could be cured by a surgical
operation.

ABLE
The doctors don't advise it. There's danger of a
stroke. I've a weak heart.

MANAGER
[*lifting the letter*]
Poor you! This letter from your last employer says
before the accident you were clean, punctual, efficient,
intelligent and popular with colleagues and superiors.

ABLE
[*eagerly*]
I loved my work. I was a quality controller.

MANAGER
It says that after it you grew slovenly, depressed

and left without giving notice.

[*She stares at* ABLE *who shrugs, sighs and shake his head.)*

## MANAGER
Tell me about your accident. I thought hyperactivity was an inherited disease.

## ABLE
Not in my case! The doctors say that if I ever have a child it's as likely to be as normal as anyone else's. About my accident . . . [*shows his knapsack*] Do you mind if I sit on a small stool I have here? I'll talk easier on it than in that .   . . thing. [*waves hand at wheelchair*]

## MANAGER
Sit how you like.

[ABLE *swiftly unpacks, unfolds and squats down on stool.*]

## ABLE
[*speaking quickly*]
I didn't always hate wheelchairs. Perhaps this happened because I liked my first one too much. I was crossing a busy road one day when the wheels jammed just as a hundred-ton juggernaut tanker came roaring round a corner. Suddenly I was up and running for the kerb. I didn't decide to do it, I just did it! And even now I can't pretend I'm sorry.

## MANAGER
That's understandable.

ABLE

[*gratefully*]

Thank you madam. The tanker crushed my chair into a knot of flattened tubes while I stood on the kerb in a crowd of folk who sat staring at me like statues. All they could do was stare – they couldn't help me! I hated that look of pity and revulsion. I ran away from them. I ran all the way home. My wife fainted when I walked in through the door.

MANAGER
[*puzzled*]
Walked?

ABLE

Crawled, I should have said. If the insurance company meets my claim I'll get a home with a six-foot high ceiling and matching door.

MANAGER

So your hyperactivity is basically a chair-phobia unfitting you for professional desk jobs.

[ABLE *becomes so excited that he has difficulty not standing up.*]

ABLE

No madam! Not at all! When working at my desk I forgot all about chairs and legs and other stupid things. I thought of nothing but quality control. I lost myself in quality control.

MANAGER

Then why did you leave Rock Fire Life? You weren't sacked.

Because of teabreaks. When teabreaks came I had
to stand up and walk about – couldn't stop myself.
That wasn't a crime, of course, but people who had
been my friends began acting as if hyperactivity was
an infectious disease: turning their faces away and
not hearing when I spoke to them. One morning I
felt unable to face them. I stayed in bed, pulled the
duvet over my head, refused to eat, drink or speak
until an ambulance took me to hospital.

### MANAGER
Sad. You were medicated?

### ABLE
With antidepressants. They made me more
depressed than ever.

### MANAGER
Did you see a psychiatrist?

### ABLE
Yes. He said it was all caused by inadequate wheel
training in infancy. It's true that I stopped crawling
later than most children – but so do forty-five per
cent of normal kids.

### MANAGER
Other therapies?

### ABLE
I was locked in a padded cell with nothing but a
wheelchair and a floor they could electrify. They tried
conditioning me into thinking the chair was a friend
because when on it I was safe from shocks through

the floor. They failed! [He gives a small frantic laugh.]I
knelt on that chair, stood, jumped up and down, danced
on it, did everything on it but sit!


### MANAGER
[*shaking head*]
Bad!


### ABLE
I was in hospital for over two years, then my wife
decided it was doing me no good and brought me
home. Luckily she's a trained nurse. She gave up
her job to look after me.


### MANAGER
Brave woman.


### ABLE
Yes, it was she who restored me to sanity. I'll always
be grateful, though she divorced me six months ago.


### MANAGER
Another man?


### ABLE
That wasn't the reason she gave. She said I would
be better on my own – that I was taking advantage
of her support to enjoy my hyperactivity.


### MANAGER
[*sternly*]
Were you?


[ABLE *does not reply but covers face with hands.*]

### MANAGER

Telling the truth won't hurt you with me, Mr
McMann. Secrecy will.

### ABLE
*[from behind his hands]*
You may find this hard to believe, but it is easier
for a man to urinate while standing up. She caught
me doing it.

### MANAGER
Anything else?

### ABLE
*[uncovering his face and sighing]*
I found it easier to sleep at nights if I danced a wee
jig round the living-room when she wasn't there.
Unluckily our house – her house – is semi-detached.
The neighbours heard me and told her. That was the
last straw – I had to leave. I learned she had another
man after my social worker helped me into a bedsit.
*[suddenly eager]* But now I'm all right! As right as I'll
ever be. All I want – all I need – is work. Something to do.
A purpose in life.

### MANAGER
*[clearing throat]*
Unluckily we cannot offer you anything as grand
as a desk in quality control but we have a vacancy
for an internal courier.

### ABLE
I'll fill it.

### MANAGER
The wage is not large.

ABLE

Anything's better than nothing.

MANAGER

But the messenger will have to use a chair.
[*She points.*]
That chair!

ABLE

[*after a pause*]

Let me tell you something madam. Using my own two feet I can do that job faster than a messenger in a chair. Chairs are faster in the open air but indoors – in a building with lots of lifts and awkward corners – you cannae beat a pair of working legs.

MANAGER

But the doors!

ABLE

I'd wear a safety helmet.

MANAGER

That is not the point, Mr McMann. My other employees will put up with your prancings if I order them but think of customers! Some are old enough to remember when people like you were never seen in public – they were doped to the eyeballs and kept in locked wards. A successful firm must not be suspected of encouraging hyperactivity. But something you said makes me think that with a little effort you can be a normal courier here.

ABLE

What did I say?

## MANAGER

That when doing a job you forgot your phobia and became lost in the job itself. So let's try a little experiment. Stand and take this letter.

[MANAGER *offers letter,* ABLE *uneasily stands, takes it.*]

## MANAGER

Imagine that I have told you to take that very important letter to our archives on the third floor – by chair of course. You have gone in your chair to the lift, entered it and pressed the third-floor button. The journey by lift takes ten seconds. Will you sit down in that chair and imagine you are carrying a letter for me while I count up to ten?

## ABLE
*[terrified]*
I . . . I . . . All right.

[ABLE *goes to the chair, takes a deep breath, closes his eyes and sits abruptly down with tightly folded arms. The* MANAGER *watching the dial of her wristwatch, steadily counts.*]

## MANAGER

One. Two. Three. Four. Five. Six. Seven . . . Eight . . . Nine . . . You've arrived!

[*She looks at* ABLE *whose face – because he is holding his breath – has gone very red.* ABLE *remains as he was, rigid with tight shut eyes.*]

## MANAGER
*[slightly worried]*
Mr McMann. Mr McMann, the game is over.

[ABLE *still does not move.* MANAGER, *more worried still,
reaches for the telephone.* ABLE *suddenly opens his
eyes and jumps up shouting:*]

### ABLE
I counted another ten!

### MANAGER
[*stretching out a firm, genial hand*]
You can do it. Join National Equilibrium tomorrow.

### ABLE
[*shaking her hand*]
God bless your madam! God bless you!

[*He dances a joyful little jig. The* MANAGER *sits down.*]

### MANAGER
[*reprovingly*]
Mr McMann!

### ABLE
[*standing still*]
Yes?

### MANAGER
Keep that sort of exercise for the privacy of home.

### ABLE
[*subdued*]
Yes madam. Thank you for reminding me madam.

### MANAGER
My name [*settles back in her chair*] is Isabel
Townsend so my employees call me Eye Tee – sounds
more democratic than madam, eh?

ABLE

Oh yes madam, – sorry madam – Eye Tee I mean.

MANAGER

Remember that part of your wage will be paid by the British taxpayer. An old-fashioned socialist would say we were exploiting you, so you needn't be so pathetically grateful to me all the time.

ABLE
*[folding stool and putting it in knapsack]*
Thank you very much for telling me that, Eye Tee. It's a great weight off my mind – thank you very, very much, Eye Tee.

*[The* MANAGER *smiles for the only time in the play.]*

# 3: OFFICE PARTY

CAST : ABLE, MANAGER, UNDERMANAGER a conventional older man wearing bright paper hat, WAITRESS, BETTY our heroine, BETH, SANDY, ALEX who fancies himself as a ladies man and wears flambouyant waistcoat. LIZ and LEX who do not speak but dance splendidly . All wear paper hats.

*The stage is meant to be a corner of a dance floor so everyone enters or leaves from front left. Dance music.* ABLE, *in wheelchair, sits backstage left watching enviously.* LEX *and* LIZ *dance on in their chairs: they are a good-looking couple in perfect harmony and obviously delighted with each other.* BETH *and* SANDY *dance in: a couple who amuse each other but are certainly not in love. They circle the stage with* LIZ *and* LEX. ALEX *rolls on, scowls at* ABLE *then goes and sits front right, watching the women dancers with the air of an experienced man assessing his chances.* BETTY *dances in with* UNDERMANAGER, *an older man who finds her attractive but to whom she is only polite.* ALEX *at once recognizes her as his target;* ABLE *also quickly notices her but at once becomes withdrawn and stops watching anyone.* MANAGER, *with glass of wine, enters and sits front left watching the company as music and dance come to an end.* LIZ *and* LEX *go to one side of the floor and sit whispering.* UNDERMANAGER *separates from* BETTY *to join* MANAGER, BETTY *and* BETH *join each other near* ABLE. WAITRESS *enters with glasses on a tray and serves them to the company starting with* ABLE, *who takes and nurses a glass of orange.*

## ALEX
[*slapping* SANDY's *back*]
Congratulations! You're well on the way with that
one. Stick it into her.

## SANDY
[*good humouredly*]
Don't be daft, she's a married woman.

## ALEX
No obstacle man! No obstacle! Who's that stotter
she's with?

## SANDY
She's just been promoted from sales into cost analysis.

## ALEX
If she was oiled the right way she'd take off like a
rocket. Slàinte!

[*Both take drinks from the waitress and sit watching*
BETTY.]

## BETTY
Thank God that's over! Why am I always picked on
by old men in senior management?

## BETH
Because you keep saying no to young ones on our level.

## BETTY
Can you wonder? Look at that pair eyeing us up.

## BETH
The one with the fancy waistcoat obviously thinks
he's your destiny.

BETTY
He'd be a fate worse than death – utter boredom.

MANAGER
[*loudly*]
Hello Able!

[*Silence.* Able *looks quickly up.*]

MANAGER
Enjoying the party, Able?
[Able *smiles, nods, raises his glass
then sips from it.*]

MANAGER
Good! Good!

[*Everybody is now looking at* Able *except the*
Waitress, *from whom the* Undermanager *takes a
glass of wine.* Lex *whispers to* Liz.]

BETTY
[*to* Beth]
I like the look of him.

BETH
Same here! I wouldnae mind a plateful myself if
he wasnae –

[Beth *leans nearer* Betty *and whispers.*]

ALEX
[*grinning*]
Did you hear the story about the hyperactive Jew,
the hyperactive lesbian, the hyperactive darkie and

the hyperactive nun who were shipwrecked on a desert island? On the first day –

SANDY
Quieter! Eye Tee is a Catholic.

[ALEX *leans nearer* SANDY *and whispers.*]

MANAGER
How's he coping?

UNDERMANAGER
[*shrugging*]
As a courier there's nothing wrong with him.

MANAGER
But?

UNDERMANAGER
Same bother we had with the last one. When not working he won't sit. If I turn round to give an order I expect a friendly human face, not a horrible blank crotch. And during teabreaks people can't talk to him without looking up at angles that are sore on the neck.

MANAGER
He stands through teabreaks?

UNDERMANAGER
Only when he thinks nobody notices, but sooner or later they do notice of course.

MANAGER
How often?

UNDERMANAGER
At least once a week.

MANAGER
That isn't often.

UNDERMANAGER
It doesn't bother me, Eye Tee, but knowing that
sooner or later they're bound to see him in that state
makes the middle management nervous.

MANAGER
Tell them that their nervousness makes him
nervous,which makes it harder for him to control
his attacks.

UNDERMANAGER
Will do, Eye Tee.

BETTY
[*to* BETH]
Hyperactivity isn't a crime – it doesn't bother me.
[*she goes to* ABLE *and sits beside him.*]

BETTY
Can I have the next dance?

ABLE
Eh . . ? Er, I don't dance I'm afraid.

BETTY
Have you never danced?

ABLE
Yes, but I had an accident.

BETTY
Hyperactivity?

ABLE
Aye.

BETTY
Why should that stop ye? You obviously still know
how to manage a chair.

ABLE
Well, if you want to know the truth . . . whenever I hear
the music I get an impulse to dance with my legs!

[BETTY *laughs cheerfully. After a moment* ABLE
*laughs too.*]

ABLE
Yes, it's funny but it's true!

BETTY
Tell you what, dance with me! I'm strong. I'll hold
ye down if you try anything outrageous.

ABLE
[*attracted*]
Will you?

ALEX
[*disgusted*]
For fuck's sake why is she chatting up him? What
use is he to her?

SANDY
Maybe she's the motherly type.

ALEX

Blethers – she's the sexy type. She's just trying to
attract attention. Well, she's got all of mine.

[*He glowers at* BETTY *and* ABLE *who are approached by the* WAITRESS.]

### WAITRESS
Another orange juice sir?

### ABLE
[*returning his glass*]
I'll risk something stronger this time.

### MANAGER
Mrs Mackintosh of material output is leaving to have a baby at the end of the month. I'm going to give her desk to Able.

### UNDERMANAGER
[*surprised*]
Can he handle it?

### MANAGER
He once handled quality control for Rock Fire Life – was a bit of a whizz kid at it. He'll easily handle material output for half Mackintosh's wage – AND without grumbling about overtime. [*She speaks very loudly.*] Good news ladies and gentlemen!

[*Everyone falls silent and stares at her.*]

### MANAGER
I'm leaving now. I know that mice play better when the cat isn't watching.

ALEX, SANDY, LEX
Hahahahahaha!

BETH, LIZ
Teeheeheehee!

*[The UNDERMANAGER registers approval by smiling
and silently clapping hands. ABLE and BETTY
exchange glances.]*

MANAGER
*[heartily]*
Goodnight Able! Goodnight Miss Macrae!

*[She leaves.]*

VOICE OFF
Take your parters for the next dance – the (dance is
named)!

*[LIZ and LEX swing onto the floor followed by
UNDERMANAGER who has gone for BETH, and BETTY
and excited ABLE. ALEX glowers at them.]*

ALEX
For fuck's sake!

SANDY
Calm down, calm down.

*[Music. The dance begins. ABLE and BETTY do very
well, and are starting to enjoy each other thoroughly
when they pass near or pause briefly near ALEX, who
speaks in a voice not loud enough to be heard by
other dancers.]*

*SCENE* Currying favour with the senior management's pet
*THREE* are we Miss Macrae?

[*After a moment of astonishment* ABLE *leaps to his feet. The other dancers stop and stare. He stands rigid with clenched fists.* ALEX, *smiling, turns away.*]

SANDY
[*to* ALEX, *muttering*]
That wasnae very nice.

BETTY
[*to* ABLE, *pleading*]
Ignore him! Sit down! Sit down!

Andrew Dawson as
that Alex

# 4 : MACRAE LIVINGROOM

CAST : ABLE, BETTY, MRS MACRAE Betty's
mother, MR MACRAE Betty's father

ABLE *and* BETTY, *partly undressed, embrace on
hearthrug in light of standard lamp, his wheelchair
on one side, hers on other. Discarded clothes – blouse,
sweater, socks, shoes – lie near. A low sideboard has
decanter and glasses. Recent lovemaking has left
them at peace together with* BETTY'S *head resting on*
ABLE'S *arm.*

### ABLE
[*after a pause*]
Are you comfortable?

### BETTY
Yes. Are you?

### ABLE
Never more so. Except I'm terrified of your mum
and dad coming back.

### BETTY
[*amused*]
Relax! They've gone to a show that won't have
reached the first interval yet.

[*She kisses him.*]

### ABLE
[*amazed and happy*]
I'm comfortable all the time with you – just seeing
you in the company corridors makes me feel at home
there. I've never felt that way with anyone else –

[ABLE *continued*]

not even before my accident. I was engaged to be married for a year and half the time my fiancée and I were quarrelling – when we weren't making love.

### BETTY
What did you quarrel about?

### ABLE
She didn't like my friends, ideas, the way I dressed or anything else about me, but that didn't stop us marrying. Betty, I'm glad my chair jammed!

### BETTY
Same here! But I hope – [*she kisses him lightly*] – I hope you're not going to propose marriage.

[*She is teasing. After a pause he speaks coldly.*]

### ABLE
Of course not. I know this is too good to last.

### BETTY
A couple should practise living together before they sign a contract to do it till one of them dies.

### ABLE
[*amazed and happy again*]
You'd like that?

[BETTY *smiles and nods.*]

### ABLE
Come here!
[*They kiss.*]

But we mustn't rush things – we must plan them very carefully.

## ABLE

I know! [*He sighs*] I wish your parents liked me. I wish you hadn't told them I was hyperactive. They wouldn't have noticed at first. They would have taken me for an ordinary bloke who's clumsy with chairs. Through knowing you I've almost overcome my phobia – I can sit down even when I'm not working, if you're nearby.

## BETTY

If I'm not ashamed of your disability why should you be, you idiot? Kiss me!

[*He is about to do so when there is a sound offstage. They sit up, staring at each other.*]

## BETTY
The car!

## ABLE
They're back.

[*He jumps up.*]

## BETTY
[*sliding into her chair*]
Sit down! Sit down! Quick! Quick!

[*She pulls on her discarded clothing.* ABLE *scoops up shoes and clothing, flops into his chair and makes a bad job of dressing himself while*

*remaining seated. Sound of door opening, then* MRS
MACRAE *rolls in and glares at* ABLE *who is pulling a
sweater over his head.* MR MACRAE *enters, more
quizzical than angry.*]

### MRS MACRAE
[*to her husband*]
I was right! I was right! "Trust Betty," you say, "Trust
Betty," and look at the state they're in! Guilt written
all over them!

### MR MACRAE
Mary, getting excited won't help.

[*Having adjusted her clothes* BETTY *folds her arms
and stares at her parents grimly.*]

### MRS MACRAE
[*to her husband*]
Oh yes I'm the unreasonable one, always
hysterical, always in the wrong, but where did
reason get us? "I'm bringing a pal home Saturday
night," says Betty – the night she knows we're
going out – "What pal?" says I. "Oh just a poor
hyperactive friend I met at work," says she –

### BETTY
[*infuriated*]
I never called him poor!

### MRS MACRAE
You implied it!

### MR MACRAE
Mary dear –

[*to* BETTY, *ignoring him*]
You can't pull wool over MY eyes Miss Reasonable! I
knew what would happen. It ruined the show for me.
We left before the interval and now the whole weekend
and everything is ruined! Everything! Ruined!

#### MR MACRAE
Mary dear –

#### MRS MACRAE
You're all obviously trying to turn me into a
hypermaniac like him!

[*She points at* ABLE. *He jumps up and recklessly
finishes dressing on his legs.*]

#### MRS MACRAE
Look at that! He isn't even trying to act normal!
[*She weeps.*]

#### ABLE
[*stooping to finish tying shoelaces*]
I'm leaving, Betty.

#### BETTY
Sit down Able! This is my house as much as theirs.
I've paid my share in it since I went to work eight
years ago.

[ABLE *sits, grabbing the arms to hold himself down.*]

#### MR MACRAE
No need to take that tone Betty but yes, stay there
Able. I want a word with you. And Mary, the world

isn't coming to an end bcause Betty and Able have snogged on the livingroom floor –

[*He lays a hand on wife's shoulder: she shakes it off.*]

## MR MACRAE
– sex isn't the life-or-death business it was in our young day, and they'd have been in her bedroom behind a locked door if they'd been up to anything serious.

## MRS MACRAE
[*becoming deadly calm*]
Having a hypermanic grandchild forced on us may not seem serious to you but I'm not having it – oh!

[*She shrieks because* ABLE, *unable to stop himself, has jumped up again. All three stare at him.*]

## MRS MACRAE
Good night! I'm going to bed. [*exits with dignity*]

[BETTY *looks anxiously at* ABLE *who stands glowering at the floor.* MR MACRAE *rolls to the sideboard saying:*]

## MR MACRAE
I need a drink after all that. Want a drink Able?

## ABLE
[*not looking at him*]
No.

## MR MACRAE
[*pouring a drink*]
I cannot deny that my wife has a temper. So has my

daughter, but I don't suppose you've seen that side of our Betty yet, Able?

### BETTY
[*fiercely*]
Keep out of this, Dad! What's between Able and me is not your business!

### MR MACRAE
Right, Betty! Health to both of you. [*raises his glass and sips*] But perhaps I love my daughter as much as you do Able, so I'd like to know your plans.

### BETTY
[*still fiercely*]
Able and I are going to live together till we find if we want to marry.

### MR MACRAE
Starting when? And where? In a bedsit? Or will you take out a mortgage on a place of your own? How are you off financially, Able? I gather you're on probation with the firm after a long spell of unemployment.

[ABLE *shifts his feet and opens his mouth to speak but* BETTY *gets in first.*]

### BETTY
Able came here to see me, not to be interrogated by you, Dad!

### MR MACRAE
[*soothingly, to* BETTY]
Let Able get a word in edgeways – I'm sure he can speak for himself.

ABLE

*[shrugging]*

I've recently been promoted to a desk job and the boss has gone out of the way to say she likes my performance. Also my insurance claim must be met sometime. My lawyers are quite confident that they'll win – the case has dragged on for five years. I used up my savings fighting it so my parents are lending me theirs.

MR MACRAE

What's the problem?

ABLE

*[sighing]*

The company who made my chair claim that it jammed because it hadn't been properly serviced – it had been, but the firm servicing it went out of business soon after. We keep finding witnesses to support my claim and the company keeps finding experts to discredit them, so each year the cost goes up. Just now my lawyers are claiming fifty thousand. If they win I'll get half that when I've met outstanding fees and repaid parents and Social Welfare.

BETTY

Insurance companies want claimants to die before a settlement is reached! Only the rich can afford lawyers who settle things fast.

MR MACRAE

*[reasonably]*

If companies met every reasonable-looking claim they would go bankrupt, Betty.

They don't say that in their adverts.

### MR MACRAE

Of course not – business is business. I'm going to ask one thing of you both – don't rush things. Plan what you do very carefully beforehand.

### BETTY
[*through gritted teeth*]
We'd decided that before Mum and you charged in!

### MR MACRAE
Yes, you've your mother's temper. I'm off to bed.

[MR MACRAE *puts down the glass, rolls to the exit but turns before leaving.*]

### MR MACRAE
Will you have children if things pan out all right?

### BETTY
[*immediately*]
Yes! – [*she hesitates*] if Able wants them too.

[*She looks appealingly at* ABLE *who smiles back then speaks more boldly than we have ever heard him.*]

### ABLE
There's no medical reason why our children will not be as fit as anyone else's, Mr Macrae.

### MR MACRAE
No medical reason, but socially they won't find life easy.

**BETTY**

The best start in life children can have is a couple of parents who love each other!

**MR MACRAE**

Oh yes, if you can love each other better than most married couples it just might compensate your weans for feeling ashamed of their father.

[ABLE *and* BETTY *stare at him.*]

**BETTY**
You're a devil, Dad!

**MR MACRAE**
*[leaving]*
Expect the worst and you'll never be disappointed Betty. Good night.

[*He leaves.* ABLE *looks at* BETTY. *She holds out her arms to him. He gets up and goes to her.*]

**ABLE**
I'm glad you want kids.
**BETTY**
*[leaving her chair for the hearthrug]*
Oh I do!

[*They find comfort by resting, clothed, in each other's arms.*]

**ABLE**
*[after a pause – wistfully]*
Have you noticed nobody minds what wee kids do with their legs? They can kick with them, stand on

them, even toddle on them before they're wheel-
trained. If they do it in public folk just smile or shrug
their shoulders.

                    BETTY
                  [*sensibly*]
They also yell and girn when hungry and wet and
mess their nappies.

                    ABLE
But working legs are a sign of healthy growth, Betty!
Won't you be glad when you feel our baby kicking
inside you?

                    BETTY
                  [*amused*]
Yes but how far back do you want to go, Able? Will
you be climbing into the trees next?

                    ABLE
                  [*chuckles*]

                    BETTY
                [*suddenly fierce*]
My dad really is a devil! We won't disappoint each
other . . . will we?

                    ABLE
             [*supremely confident*]
                We'll get on fine.

# 5 : SEVERAL PLACES

CAST : A PRIME MINISTER, MANAGER,
SOCIAL WORKER, ABLE

*Total Darkness*
ANNOUNCER'S VOICE
And now, an election address by the Prime Minister
of Britain, the Right Honourable Humpty Dipsy.

*A spotlight shows the* MINISTER *seated centrestage
and facing the air above the audience's heads with
an expression of indomitable courage. He wears a
white hospital gown, glasses with black lenses and
a hearing aid. From an attachment to his chair a
tube runs from a suspended bottle into a bandage
on his arm. He carefully unplugs his hearing aid
and clasps hands on crossed legs before speaking.*

PRIME MINISTER
Good evening. All political parties seek election by
promising to make life better for people, and there
was once a time when British governments did it
by pampering minorities. The strong and efficient
were penalized to benefit the feeble and useless;
good, successful workers were taxed to make life
easy for those who could not or would not work. You
all know what that led to. British employers could
not compete in foreign markets, teenagers turned
to sexual promiscuity, drug abuse was advocated
by trendy artists and gurus and even a
parliamentary commission! No wonder that the
British people decided to call a halt.

You did it by electing into government a party

which promised to get Britain rolling forward
instead of continually applying brakes and letting
air out of our tyres. My party kept these promises,
which is why we have been in power ever since. Yes,
some people are homeless but more Britons than
ever occupy homes of their own. This is good for
them, good for our banks, good for our building
societies. Yes, inadequate people whinge about the
state of public healthcare, but those with thrift and
foresight face the future without fear because
London is insurance capital of the world. Most
Britons today are tougher, more independent, more
realistic and – as MPs of every party realize – more
wealthy than they have been since the great days
of the Empire. And if you don't like how we have
achieved this you won't change it by voting for
others! Those who attacked our curbs on trade union
and local government dictatorship, those who fought
our sale of public transport, communications, power,
heat and water, now admit that our good work
cannot be undone, so no matter who takes office
after us, we will have conquered.

So with full confidence in the support of the
majority I announce a new round of tax cuts, to be
paid for by the total privatization of property and
services remaining in public hands. I know this will
cause the usual outcry about the plight of the
unemployed, the aged and the hyperactive poor, but
remember the words of Saint Paul: "Now abideth
Faith, Hope and Charity, and the greatest of these is
Charity." Which is why Charity – like banking,
insurance and arms manufacture – is another British
industry in a healthy and flourishing condition. I am
sorry for the unemployed, the elderly and the
hyperactive poor, but my job is still to get as many

IAN HAMILTON *as the* RIGHT HONOURABLE HUMPTY DIPSY

as possible rolling forward at their own speed on their own wheels. Goodnight.

[*The spotlight goes out and reappears left on the* MANAGER *who is dictating a letter.*]

### MANAGER

Dear Mr McMann, when you joined this firm I told you that the welfare subsidy was a great part of what made it profitable to employ you. Since this subsidy is terminating I am compelled to give you a month's notice. I regret it because you have been a highly valued member of my staff; but Mrs Mackintosh returns at the end of the month having recovered from her pregnancy. If I scrapped her instead of you I might be charged with wrongful dismissal. Your old post of courier has of course been filled.

43

SEVERAL

I enclose a reference stating that your ability, PLACES
efficiency and willingness to serve are exceptional, and
that your physical condition in no way disqualifies
you for a desk at the highest level of middle
management. Why not use this reference to get
yourself off the hyperactivity register? My influence –
and perhaps a young lady in cost analysis – seem to
have cured you of standing up and jigging about.
Discuss it with your social worker.

[*Spotlight switches right to* ABLE *and* SOCIAL WORKER
*facing each other.* ABLE, *holding a letter, is cheerily
wheeling his chair backwards and forwards.*]

### ABLE
[*eagerly*]
See! I can use this no bother! I've got over my phobia!

### SOCIAL WORKER
Are you really cured of standing and jigging?

### ABLE
[*not embarrassed*]
Oh I do it at home! All the time! It drives the other
flat-mates mad but they're a bunch of alcies so the
landlord doesn't care. And I NEVER do it at work.

### SOCIAL WORKER
You'll be out of work in a fortnight.

### ABLE
But with this reference from Eye Tee – [*he waves it*]
– I can go to the job centre and sign on to the
professional register if I get my name off the
hyperactive one! [*he twirls his chair around.*]

SOCIAL WORKER
There's a lot more professional unemployment than the government admits. And nowadays the hyperactive register is much easier to get off than on – as you'll learn if you find work and then have a relapse.

ABLE
[*sitting still at last*]
If I thought like you do I would take seriously to drink!

SOCIAL WORKER
[*apologetic*]
Sorry Able – in my job we get used to expecting the worst, and coming off the hyperactive register is going to affect your disability allowance and insurance claim.

ABLE
[*blithely*]
I've seen my lawyers about that! They say that if I get a decent job they'll have to settle for less money, but it will be enough to pay them and pay what I owe my parents and the Social Welfare – and I'll still have a few hundred pounds to myself. The important thing is a fresh start in life!

SOCIAL WORKER
[*after a pause*]
I admire your guts, Able. Good luck. [*He holds out his hand.*] Good luck. Goodbye. You're my final case.

ABLE
[*shaking hands*]
You're leaving social work?

I'm taking early retirement. The job's become too
tough for me.

### ABLE
Can I ask something?

[SOCIAL WORKER *nods.*]

### ABLE
Why don't Welfare offices employ hyperactive social
workers to deal with hyperactive people? They
wouldn't need to ask a lot of questions because they
would understand our situation already.

### SOCIAL WORKER
Can't you work that out for yourself? [*grins bitterly*]
[ABLE *shakes his head.*]

### SOCIAL WORKER
The government doesn't want employees who
understand people like you – it wants nothing to do
with people like you. I belong to a dying breed – the
social worker who was employed to help. If you have
a relapse and come back to us you will be given a
form asking for exact details of everywhere you've
lived and everything you've done. This information
is already stored in official data banks but many
folk have forgotten it so will be eliminated because
their form is incomplete. The rest will then receive
a questionnaire which gets them assessing their own
hyperactivity through a points allocation system
which only those who invented it can understand.
And the winners of this mental obstacle race will
be sifted out by a machine – a processor which

SOCIAL WORKER [*continued*]
chooses who to benefit not according to needs, but
on the basis of funds which are slowly being reduced
to zero.

[ABLE *has grown restless during this speech.*]

ABLE
But . . . But . . .

SOCIAL WORKER
[*interrupting*]
If you want to know why the government is slowly,
not quickly axing social welfare, it's because our
middle class would be shocked if our cities suddenly
started looking like Calcutta or Jakarta with
skeletal hyperactive beggars doing dances of death
on every corner. They're being allowed time to get
used to it. Our upper classes are unshockable of
course. They live in country houses or specially
policed security zones.

ABLE
[*indignant*]
You've a sick mind! I would certainly take to drink
if I believed that Britain is going to be like that!

SOCIAL WORKER
[*soothingly*]
You needn't believe what you can't see, Able. I hope
to hell you get a decent job – and keep it!

[*spotlight goes out*]

# 6 : MACRAE LIVINGROOM

CAST:
BETTY, MRS MACRAE, ABLE, MR MACRAE

*Light comes up on* BETTY *who, distressed, sits knitting a small garment, watched tensely by her mother opposite. Voices are squabbling offstage. Voices offstage and on overlap.*

ABLE'S VOICE
I've got to see her! I've got to see her!

MR MACRAE'S VOICE
Not possible, Able.

MRS MACRAE
Pay no attention.

ABLE'S VOICE
Why won't she see me? We haven't quarrelled, and I've good news for her – for both of us. Tell me what's wrong, Mr Macrae!

MR MACRAE'S VOICE
She doesn't want to see you and that's not wrong, it's right, Able!

BETTY
I wish I could see him! [*She stops knitting.*]

MRS MACRAE
[*Hissing.*]
You promised not to!

SCENE
SIX

**ABLE'S VOICE**
Stop condescending to me, Mr Macrae! You are no longer dealing with a hyperactive invalid! I am as firmly settled in my chair as you are in yours!

**MR MACRAE'S VOICE**
If you want a fight you've found the right man!

[*Sounds of a struggle.*]

**MRS MACRAE**
[*swivelling her chair*]
I'm phoning the police!

**BETTY**
No!

**ABLE'S VOICE**
[*shouting*]
Betty, are you there? I'm off the hyperactive register and I've a new job! A great new job!

**BETTY**
[*shouting*]
Able! Able! Oh let him in Dad! Please! Please! Please!

[*She weeps.* ABLE *rolls in, embraces and comforts her.* MR MACRAE *enters more slowly. Both men are untidy from their tussle.*]

**MRS MACRAE**
[*violently, to her husband*]
You had no right to let that man into our house! No right! None at all! You promised you wouldn't so fling him out! Fling him out!

MR MACRAE
[*patiently*]
Mary . . .

MRS MACRAE
Fling him out now! Now! Now!

MR MACRAE
Mary, you can see Able has taken to his wheels like
a duck to water, and if he has a good job . . . What
job is it, Able?

ABLE
Managing the supply department of Caledonian
Gubernators – more responsibility and better wages
than I had with Rock Fire Life.

MR MACRAE
That's a better job than I ever had, Mary, so we
haven't an axle to revolve on.

BETTY
[*drying her eyes*]
Leave Able and me alone for a bit, both of you. I've
some explaining to do.

MR MACRAE
[*going*]
True. Come on Mary.

MRS MACRAE
[*following him out, weeping*]
Oh it's not fair. Not fair. After all I did for that girl
– after all I was going to do for her – everybody's
ganged up against me again.

Mary Hamilton
Betty as Macrae

ABLE
What was the matter?

BETTY
Do you know what this is? [*She displays knitting
with partly finished article of baby wear.*]

ABLE
[*delighted*]
A baby?
[*She smiles and nods. They embrace.*]

ABLE
[*amused*]
We did so little!

BETTY
It was enough.

ABLE
You thought you were in a safe period!

BETTY
Yes, it was me who led you on after deciding to be
slow and careful. Then National Equilibrium fired
you and I was afraid you'd feel I'd trapped you.

ABLE
Poor Betty!

BETTY
I didn't know what to do. Dad wanted me to
terminate it . . .

ABLE
The bastard!

BETTY
Luckily Mum was on my side – in a way. She said
I must have the baby and live here and she'd look
after both of us – if I promised not to see you again.

ABLE
The bitch!

BETTY
She meant well. She'll adjust to us when we get our
own house in a nice neighbourhood, and we will,
won't we? We'll easily get a mortgage now, won't
we?

ABLE
Yes. I'm starting on Monday as a supplies manager
with a staff of seventeen under me. Happy ending!

BETTY
Happy beginning!

ACT TWO
ROAD TO RUIN

Morag McAlpine
as Meg of the
Supply Office
26 - 11 - 1991

# 7 : SUPPLY OFFICE

CAST : MEG a small dour efficient woman who says as little as possible and talks fast when forced to talk, BLAND the busines person of first scene, ABLE wearing smart business sut, waistcoat, tie.

*A telephone rings before the light goes up on centre stage with two desks. The left faces audience and holds a word processor, telephone, empty IN and OUT trays. The right desk faces the left with front edge touching. Here a word processor, both trays and every surface carry overflowing heaps of order forms, manuals and correspondence.* MEG *sits at this desk in profile to the audience, telephone handset to ear, patiently trying to soothe someone who is angry about something. While she talks* BLAND *and* ABLE *roll in but she ignores them until* BLAND *speaks to her directly.*

#### MEG
I'm sorry, I know . . . I know, I'm sorry . . . Yes, I know you should have had them today, yes we promised them today but . . .

[*enter* BLAND *and* ABLE]

#### BLAND
Here it is, your new dominion, the nerve centre of Scottish gubernator supply.

#### MEG
. . . no, sorry, no I can't promise delivery tomorrow though I'll do my best, sorry, goodbye. [*She puts the phone down and taps rapidly on the word processor.*]

BLAND

[*indicating* MEG]

This is Meg, your assistant, who has been with us for twenty years. She knows more about gubernator supply than anyone else here – even me! Especially me, whose grandfather started the business! Isn't that right Meg?

MEG

[*pausing with fingers on keyboard*]
Yes?

BLAND

You know more about this business than anyone else. Right?

MEG

Yes! [*She resumes typing.*]

BLAND

Not so fast! Meet Able McMann, your new boss. Put him in the picture. Show him the grips. Teach him the moves Meg and don't be too hard on him.

[MEG *folds arms, looks expressionlessly at* ABLE.]

ABLE

[*trying to be nice*]
I'm very glad to meet you.

MEG

Hullo.

BLAND

Good, I'll leave both you to get on with it. [*produces*

*cigarette case*] I'll have a word with Dimitri Suave
of foreign orders, a tremendous character, the life
and soul of any party. I'll come back later to see
how you're doing and make some suggestions . . .

[*He pauses to light a cigarette. The phone rings.* MEG *lifts it.*]

### MEG
Yes? . . . No, I'm sorry . . . I'm sorry, I know . . . Yes
I know we promised them for last week but . . .

### BLAND
[*Talking loudly over her.*]
Learn all you can from Meg but don't let her bully you!
Our last supplies chief was so wholly under her thumb
that we had to let him go – he didn't last a fortnight.
Remember, the buck stops with you! Bye bye!

[*Exit* BLAND. ABLE *faces* MEG.]

### MEG
. . . I'm sorry, I can't promise a definite delivery
date before the consignment leaves our depot, but
I'll do my best. . . . I'm sorry, that's all I can do.

[*She puts phone down and faces* ABLE.]

### MEG
Welcome to hell.

[ABLE *stares at her.*]

### MEG
I said welcome to hell.

ABLE

[*going behind the left desk*]
You're obviously telling me something but I need an explanation. [*Awaits explanation, arms folded on desktop.*]

MEG
[*sighing*]
I'll make it short and simple. We're a long-established Scottish firm which supplies things a lot of people want, but we're losing business to an English competitor with one advantage over us.

ABLE
Superior technology?

MEG
No.

ABLE
Better advertising?

MEG
No.

ABLE
Competitive underpricing?

MEG
No. Their senior management in London lets their Scottish management get on with the job. Our Senior Management Group – I call them the Smug – draw big salaries for doing sweet damn nothing. I don't mind that. It is a fact of life that the least productive people get the most money. But our Smug

aren't content with money, they feel insecure if they
aren't issuing commands, so they give folk like you and me – especially folk like me – instructions which make efficiency impossible.

ABLE
That can't be the whole story.

MEG
Then forget it. Would you sign these supply forms? I can't authorize them now you're here. [*Offers him a fat sheaf of papers.*]

ABLE
[*not taking them*]
Have you checked them? Are they in order?

MEG
Yes.

ABLE
You could issue them when I wasn't here?

MEG
Yes, between bosses it's me who issues them.

ABLE
Then I – your present boss – don't want to waste time signing them. Send them out as they are.

MEG
[*with a pitying shake of the head*]
Sorry boss. If I do that the Smug will say I've taken over your job and you – not me! – will be reprimanded.

[ABLE *takes the forms and with gloomy rapidity signs and piles them up while* MEG *taps briskly on her keyboard. These activities continue as they talk.*]


### ABLE

It strikes me . . . that the Smug . . . should have given you my job.


### MEG
[*nodding*]
Yes.


### ABLE

Did they not do it because you're a woman?


### MEG

They didn't do it because they knew I would tell them to their faces what I've told them for years through interior memoranda which they ignore.


### ABLE

Why did my predecessor only last a fortnight?


### MEG

He was conscientious. He tried to improve things.

[*The phone rings on* MEG's *desk.*]


### ABLE

I'll handle it! [*He lifts his phone with the left hand and continues signing with the right.*] Yes, supplies here . . . I'm sorry, I didn't know . . . Yes, I can well believe it . . . No I cannot give you a new delivery date because though I am head of supplies I only started work today and have not yet come to grips

with some hitches generated by what I am told is a
new computer programme, but rest assured that
your problem is now top of the Caledonian
Gubernator priority list. Good day.

> MEG
> [*impressed, but still typing*]
> Well done. Who was it?

> ABLE
> [*Still busily signing*]
> Clapperclaw Service Stations.

> MEG

Poor souls! They're ninth on our priority list. I wish
the government hadn't scrapped the hyperactive
welfare scheme. It would save us time and money
to have a cheap hyperactive sitting in a cubicle doing
nothing but apologize over the phone. Something
wrong?

[*She looks at* ABLE *who now scowls at the forms in
front of him, tapping them steadily with the end of
his pen. She stops typing.*]

> MEG
> Is something wrong?

> ABLE
> [*abruptly*]

The woman I love is pregnant and lives with her
parents. I live in a bedsit not much bigger than a
cubicle in a house full of sick and elderly people. I
want to marry, get a nice home, support a family. I
need this job. How can I keep it?

MEG

[*shrugging*]

Easy. Don't do a damn thing except suck up to the senior management. Pass on their orders to your underlings without question and when chaos follows blame us for it. Entertain the Smug with all sorts of stories about our stupidity and incompetence. Never never never suggest that they change their ways. They'll think you one of them and your future here will be secure – as long as the firm lasts. I give it three years at the most. [*She sighs.*] And now if I can attend to my work I may achieve a miracle – six thousand double-elephant gubernators delivered to Alpha Index of Coventry on time today. They're the only big company which still has faith in us and please! Finish signing these forms.

[*She types,* ABLE *signs. Enter* BLAND, *very cheerful.*]

BLAND

Busy busy busy are we? Good good good. There is something you can do for me, Able. I've just had a phone call from Sir Arthur Shots, a very gallant old soldier and near cousin of Humpty Dipsy. Though three score and ten he still plays his regular eighteen holes round the Royal and Ancient and his golfchair needs a new gubernator. Knowing I am in the business he has asked me to send one fast without using the normal boring supply channels. He only needs one wee small tiny semi-demi gubernator of the sort we supply to Clapperclaw Service Stations and Clapperclaw are not fast deliverers –

ABLE

I know why; you see we –

Allow me to finish. What you KNOW is less
important than what you DO, so tell Meg to stop
what she's doing and give top priority to Arthur
Shots. I hear that a truck is leaving the depot for
Coventry shortly. Get Meg to send it to St Andrews
first — she'll find Arthur's exact address in Who's
Who. It is an honour and privilege to be useful to
such a man. [*He* smiles genially at *ABLE*.]

[*MEG stops typing, folds arms, watches* ABLE
*expressionlessly.* ABLE *shuts eyes, sucks lower lip,
then opens eyes and speaks quietly but firmly.*]

### ABLE
Mr Bland, that's impossible. That truck is delivering
a huge consignment to our best client and they won't
arrive as promised if we divert it to —

[BLAND, *wagging a forefinger, interrupts more
genially than ever.*]

### BLAND
Nothing is impossible Able! Never let the word
impossible be heard within the walls of Caledonian
Gubernators! I see you have been got at by the
excellent and indispensable Miss Meg, a middle-
management pessimist who would sink us all in
gloom if ignorant males like us did not take a
broader view. Numerically speaking, yes, it is foolish
to deliver six thousand double elephants later than
promised so that one little wee tiny semi-demi is
delivered on time, but priorities are not always
governed by arithmetic. Sir Arthur is on the board
of many important companies. Clapperclaw Services

BLAND [*continued*]

and Alpha Index of Coventry could well be among
them. So! Now! Do! What! I! Say! [*He shows all his
teeth in a grin.*]

[ABLE *shuts eyes, folds arms tight, rocks to and fro.*]

### BLAND
[*sharply*]
Well?

### ABLE
[*loudly, without looking at* MEG]
Do what he says.

### MEG
[*giving a smart military salute*]
Yes sir! At once sir! I'll go and look for a Who's Who
sir!

[MEG *swings her chair round and leaves fast.*]

### BLAND
[*calling after her, laughing:*]
My secretary will give you one Meg, hahahaha!
What a weird sense of humour she has, women are
inexplicable . . . [*He looks, puzzled, at* ABLE] Is
something wrong?

[ABLE *still rocks to and fro with shut eyes, tightly
grasping the arms of his chair.*]

### BLAND
[*gently and kindly*]
You seem ill – can I do something to help?

[BLAND *lays a kindly hand on* ABLE's *arm.* ABLE *suddenly opens eyes and shows his teeth in a hysterical grin.*]

ABLE

You can do nothing to help but vanish! [*stands up*]
Disappear! [*shakes clenched fists and roars*] Fuck
off out of here!

[BLAND *recoils in terror, leaves swiftly.* ABLE *drops
back into chair and covers face with hands.*]

Forrest Alexander as Mr Bland

# 8 : BENEFIT TRIBUNAL

CAST: A, B, C and D, four deaf mute Social Workers, ABLE wearing the suit of scene 6 but less smartly, NEXT CASE with working legs but one line only.

*Front left a white circular mat 18 inches across with a black blindfold on it, the blindfold with elastic for ease of putting on and off. Back right and angled to confront the mat, a platform high enough to lift the heads of those sitting there above the head of anyone standing below. A table on the platform has* A *and* B *sitting side-by-side behind,* A *with a pushbell,* B *with an Anglepoise lamp casting strong light on the mat – other light is comparatively dim.* C *and* D *sit one at each end of the table. All four have sheaves of typed reports and printed forms on tabletop or armrest. All four are wired to an artificial voicebox in the centre of the table so in the following dialogue it is impossible to say exactly which of them is speaking. It must be one who has watched* ABLE's *lips, but two of them are always doing this, though never the same two. Throughout this scene messages are exchanged in sign language. Directions for them are given in a different typeface because they don't interrupt the dialogue though happening at the same time, and* ABLE *is not aware of it.*

*The scene starts with* A *striking the pushbell as* C *and* D *examine papers.*

### VOICEBOX
Next case – Able McMann.

[ABLE *enters left and stares down at mat and then at the tribunal, unsure what to do.*]

Stand on that spot facing the light and we'll have
no trouble reading your lips Mr McMann.

[ABLE *lifts blindfold and stands where it lay, blinking
into light of Anglepoise lamp as* B *tightens the screw
so that the beam rests on* ABLE's *face.*]

### C
[*signing to* D]
**How's your head feeling now?**

### D
[*signing back*]
**Horrible! Probably still as bad as yours.**

### A
[*signing to* C *and* D]
**Careful! Maybe he can read us.**

### VOICEBOX
Use the blindfold if the light hurts your eyes.

### ABLE
[*humbly*]
Thank you. [*puts on blindfold*] Thank you, that's a
lot better. Am I looking the right way again?

### A
[*signing to the rest*]
**We've six others to see before the break. Be
quick with this one.**

### VOICEBOX
Yes. Why are you standing there Mr McMann?

ABLE

Because soon I'll need money – soon I'll be penniless.

VOICEBOX

You find standing gets more sympathy than sitting down?

ABLE
No!

VOICEBOX

You came off the hyperactive register after holding a good desk job for six months. A recent medical report says the doctor found no muscular or nervous ailment to stop you sitting down for fourteen or fifteen hours a day – like many other hyperactives who manage to lead normal lives.

ABLE
[*hesitantly*]

Then that doctor . . . is not a good doctor . . . because he ignored what I said. I told him that when worried about the future – when terrified of the future – I stand or walk about until I drop. If he suspected me of lying he should have got one of your snoopers – sorry sorry one of your investigators – to learn the truth from my neighbours.

C
[*signing*]

**Oh we've a real Smart Alec here, haven't we? This one fancies himself as a lawyer!**

A

**He's right though. In a juster world . . .**

**We haven't the resources to be just.**

A
**But in a kinder world –**

D
**We haven't the resources to be kind.**

VOICEBOX
Our doctors are overworked, Mr McMann, and despite rumours to the contrary there is a limit to our number of investigators. You have been employed twice since you came off the hyperactive register and both times left work on your first day. Why?

ABLE
At Caledonian Gubernators I did not see eye to eye with the director –

VOICEBOX
So you resorted to menacing language.

ABLE
Only a little! I'm not a violent man – I've no record of menacing behaviour before then –

VOICEBOX
[*without pause between sentences*]
You have now why did you leave Hurricane Sales Service?

ABLE
I was shut in a room full of teenagers, young folk who don't feel it's rude and intrusive to phone

ABLE [*continued*]

housewives and elderly folk and talk them into
letting in even tougher salesmen, but I –

VOICEBOX

Felt able to pick and choose you received nineteen
thousand insurance compensation for the initial
injury of which nine thousand seven hundred and
twelve were repaid to Social Welfare leaving nine
thousand two eighty eight what became of it?

C
[*signing*]
**What chance do you think Iron Butterfly has for
the two-thirty at Uttoxeter?**

B
**Shut up! Some of us have to watch the poor
bugger's mouth.**

D
**We've seen a million poorer buggers.
Iron Butterfly hasn't a hope in hell.**

ABLE

After repaying my parents' legal expenses loan I
had less than seven hundred. I've been living on
that but I'm down to my last two hundred and will
lose my bedsit in two or three weeks if I can't get –

VOICEBOX
Won't your parents help?

ABLE
They're old people living in sheltered housing and

afraid of illness and with the National Health
Service as it is I don't want to bother them. Do you
need to ask all these questions? I've answered them
again and again in forms I've filled in several times.
Have you not read them?

### VOICEBOX
You argue very strongly for someone who wants us
to think he's in a weak position.

[ABLE *helplessly shrugs shoulders, shakes head.*]

### C
[*signing*]
**He's no answer to that one!**

### A
**But his body language is eloquent.**

### ABLE
[*appealing*]
Surely you're paid to HELP people like me – not to
make us feel guilty.

### D
[*signing*]
**Get rid of him.**

### VOICEBOX
We are paid to separate scroungers and spongers
from those who need help and deserve support. Your
aggressiveness and rejection of job opportunities
are not attitudes that deserve support. You admit
that at present you do not need help since you have
a room and money for rent. Should your material

circumstances change in the near future you have
every right to apply to us again in six weeks.
Goodbye.

[A *hits the pushbell*, B *switches the lamp off and they
converse among themselves while* ABLE *pleads on.*]

### ABLE

But if you don't give me cash I'll be homeless in six
weeks. Without a fixed address I can't apply to you
again! Your rules don't allow it. Yes I might hold on a
bit longer by begging from my parents and the woman
I love but I don't want to beg, I'd feel dirty, feel
despicable begging, don't make me a beggar please.
You seem to think I'm a tough guy but I'm not, I'm an
ordinary man who did a steady nine to five job, did
exactly what I was told, like you do! I paid taxes just
like you do for eight years before my accident. Are you
listening to me? Please? Are you?

### A
[*signing*]
**That was a tough one!**

### B
**I admired his attitude to his parents.**

### D
**If he's not a fool we've taught him a lesson which
will do him good.**

### C
**He's a fool, a bore, a snob and a weakling and we're
rid of him – thank goodness – for ever.**

**A year ago we would have helped him.**

B
**Those days have gone for ever.**

C
**Look, he's still raving at us!**

[A *looks at papers and hits the pushbell again.*]

VOICEBOX
Next applicant please – Jack O'Rourke.

ABLE
Did you not hear what I said?

[A *tough guy enters left, slaps* ABLE's *shoulder.*]

NEXT APPLICANT
My turn for the blindfold mate.

[ABLE *pulls blindfold off and stares at* NEXT
APPLICANT, *open mouthed.*]

# 9 : LOUNGE BAR

CAST : BARTENDER, THRUST, BLAND, SUAVE,
COY, MISS SHY a spinster with working legs,
ABLE, FOUR OF THE CHAIR POLICE.
*The scene is set exactly like the start of scene one,
except that* MISS SHY *crouches on a folding stool to
one side, nursing on her knee a handbag which held
the stool and trying, with small beckonings, to get
the* BARTENDER's *attention.*


THRUST

He comes from the shoot-em kill-em brigade into
contract management and doesn't even know that
a contract locks you into a fixed profit margin.

BLAND
You told me that quite a while ago.

THRUST
It still happens. Same again?

BLAND
Please.

THRUST
Bartender! Same again!

BARTENDER
Certainly sir.

SUAVE
[*intimately*]
My wife mentioned you over breakfast this morning.

Oo! What did she say?

SUAVE
"Who's that woman in your office who dresses with
unusual elegance?" I told her I knew nobody like
that in my office.

COY
[*smiling and placing her hand on his*]
You've a wild sense of humour. I could never fall for
a man who hadn't a wild sense of humour. Let's be
wicked. Let's have another.

SUAVE
Same again, bartender!

BARTENDER
In a minute sir!

THRUST
Common workmen are no trouble nowadays and
soon the skilled technicians will knuckle under too.
Who'll need them? Their work will be done by
Brazilian and Chinese orphans paid with handfuls
of food – and grateful for it.

BLAND
Thank goodness there'll always be room for our kids
in administration. My turn to pay. [*He pays*
BARTENDER *who has just served drink.*]

BARTENDER
[*calling to* SUAVE]
Two gins and tonics was it sir?

SUAVE

[*indicating* MISS SHY]
Yes but I believe this lady should be served first —
she's been waiting some time.

[MISS SHY *smiles gratefully at* SUAVE, COY *pats his
hand approvingly, he shrugs modestly.*]

BARTENDER

It's not easy to see people whose heads are not on
the usual level sir. What would you like madam?

MISS SHY

A small dry sherry if it's no trouble thank you!

[*Enter* ABLE *in a wheelchair, very fast. He wears a
dandelion flower in his lapel and hides hysterical
excitement under a cheerful manner.*]

BARTENDER

Is alcohol alright for someone in your condition?

MISS SHY
[*nodding*]
Yes! My doctor recommends it.

ABLE
[*boisterously*]
There's a voice I know! Don't worry bartender, this
lady is a friend of mine. Give her what she wants
and give me a large Glenfiddich!

BARTENDER
[*smartly*]
At once sir!

[ABLE *sits facing* MISS SHY *with his back to the rest* 77
*of the room. He speaks quietly to her at first and is* LOUNGE
*ignored by all but* BLAND.] BAR

MISS SHY
I'm sorry but I don't know you at all.

ABLE
Never mind. I hate these selfish bastards too.

MISS SHY
[*alarmed*]
I don't hate anyone, what do you mean?

ABLE
I'll show you if nobody's watching. Are they?

MISS SHY
[*looking*]
A big man over there is watching.

[ABLE *looks round then waves, smiling broadly.*]

ABLE
A fine evening Mr Bland! Do you remember me?

BLAND
[*sternly*]
Indeed I do.

ABLE
No hard feelings I hope Mr Bland?

BLAND
None! None! [*He becomes genial.*] Glad to see you

**BLAND** [*continued*]
looking so very much better. [*He turns and talks quietly to* THRUST.]

[ABLE, *seeing nobody watching now, turns back to* MISS SHY *and shoots both legs out straight for a second.*]

### MISS SHY
[*nodding gravely*]
I see.

### ABLE
[*patting his chairarm*]
I only need this contraption to get service in bars.

[BARTENDER *approaches with tray of drinks, for all.* ABLE *puts a five-pound note on his tray.*]

### ABLE
Keep the change, tonight I have something to celebrate. Do you remember me, by the way?

### BARTENDER
[*staring*]
Thank you sir but I can't say I do.

### ABLE
Forget it. [*to* MISS SHY] Yes, I'm celebrating tonight. Skol!

[ABLE *drinks.* BARTENDER *serves* SUAVE *and* COY, *but thereafter watches* ABLE *thoughtfully.*]

### MISS SHY
Are you drunk?  [*places her glass on the floor*]

Slightly. But don't worry. An hour will pass before my *LOUNGE*
condition gets me into serious trouble. [*He drinks.*] *BAR*

### MISS SHY
Oh please don't lose control! Things get much worse
if you do – I once lost control.

### ABLE
You haven't asked what I'm celebrating.

### MISS SHY
[*concerned for him*]
You mustn't lose control!

### ABLE
I am celebrating a new life. [He drinks.] After closing
time tonight I will be a new age traveller, a nomad,
gypsy, sponger, scrounger, parasite, one of Great
Britain's mighty army of homeless and hopeless.
[*more thoughtfully*] Tomorrow I may also be a father.

### MISS SHY
[*horrified*]
You should be saving every penny, not buying drink.

### ABLE
The money I am spending is rent due to a landlord
who has evicted me. If I pay him I will not only be
homeless but penniless so I am giving myself a treat
before taking to the road.

### MISS SHY
[*very quietly*]
You're frightening me.

ABLE
[*sincerely*]
I'm sorry.

BLAND
[*quietly, to* THRUST]
All the same he makes me decidedly uneasy. Let's go.

[BLAND *and* THRUST *start to go out handing their glasses to* BARTENDER *as they pass.*]

ABLE
[*boisterously*]
Leaving already Mr Bland? I hoped there would be time for another wee get-together – a friendly return match for Auld Lang Syne. You definitely beat me last time.

[BLAND *and* THRUST *leave fast.*]

ABLE
Another large malt please!

BARTENDER
Sorry sir but you've had enough.

ABLE
I'm the best judge of that –

[BARTENDER *reaches for telephone*]

ABLE
Don't touch that!

[BARTENDER *freezes, his fingers almost touching the*

*handset of a phone.* ABLE *gets up, walks swiftly*
*across, rips the handset from the wall and flings it*
*away. He then speaks to* SUAVE *and* COY *in a loud,*
*firm, sober voice:*]

### ABLE
Closing time lady and gentleman. I'm afraid I must
ask you to leave.

### SUAVE
Certainly certainly!
[*Knocking his gin back he rushes out in abject panic.*]

### COY
[*squealing and pursuing*]
You bastard, wait for me!

[MISS SHY *stands up, clutching her handbag and
weeping with pity.*]

### BARTENDER
[*grimly*]
You're in trouble – serious trouble.

[ABLE *grips back of* BARTENDER's *chair and
pushes it toward the exit saying:*]

### ABLE
So fetch the police. Tell them I haven't a gun, haven't
a knife but will put up a fight all the same – just for
laughs – just for exercise. Right?

### BARTENDER
[*rolling off*]
Right, but you really are in trouble!

[ABLE *goes to* MISS SHY, *picks up her stool, folds it
*and holds it out to her.*]

### ABLE
[*cheerfully and kindly*]
Open up!

### MISS SHY
[*weeping and shaking her head*]
You've lost control, you've lost control!

### ABLE
[*smiling*]
I honestly think I've gained it. Open up.

### MISS SHY
[*opening her handbag*]
I would like to stay with you but I'm too frightened!
Too frightened!

### ABLE
[*slipping the stool inside*]
Will you take a message for me? To my wife – I mean
to my girlfriend, Betty Macrae.

[MISS SHY *nods hard.*]

### ABLE
She's in a maternity ward of the Queen Mother's.
Tell her not to be ashamed of me because I'm not
ashamed of myself! Tell her to tell our child – when
it's old enough – that Daddy started life as a wimp
who not even hyperactivity could change. Tell Betty
that I achieved manhood through her love and the
promise of a child. Betty Macrae and my child gave

me the guts to be nasty and violent instead of
helpless and pitiable. Tell her I am now a force to
reckon with, a father to be proud of! [*raising a*
*clenched fist*]    Hypermanics of the world, unite!

[Miss Shy, *inspired, drops her bag and embraces him vigorously.*]

### MISS SHY
You're wonderful – I'm staying here!

[*They kiss fiercely then* Able *holds her away from him.*]

### ABLE
No! You must deliver my message!
[*He releases her.*]

### MISS SHY
[*Stooping for her handbag she looks up to him.*]
I will tell it to everyone!

### ABLE
[*pointing off*]
Go! And remember, walk tall!

### MISS SHY
[*standing up*]
This is the happiest moment of my life.

### ABLE
Same here!

[*As* Miss Shy *leaves, walking on tiptoe as tall as possible,* Able *dances a jig round the stage. It ends with him pushing his wheelchair off then picking up the glass of sherry.*]

### ABLE

Clear decks for action! [*He goes to bar and sits on it, pondering.*] Half an hour ago I expected to pass the night dead drunk in a cardboard box under the Monkland motorway. Now I'll pass it in a solid room with inside lavatory, clean blankets and regular big mugs of sweet hot milky tea at the taxpayer's expense. Why haven't other homeless folk discovered that option? Perhaps they have. Of course they have. It explains the soaring crime rate.

[*He drains sherry glass in one swallow, puts it down, stands, takes a larger glass in each hand, fills them from suspended gin and whisky bottles singing:*]

### ABLE

Scots wha hae wi' Wallace bled,
Scots wham Bruce has aften led,
Welcome to your gory bed
Or to victory!

[*He swallows the glass of whisky in three gulps.* Sounds *of rapidly approaching police sirens.*]

### ABLE

Now's the day and now's the hour,
See the front o' battle lour,
See approach proud Edward's power
Chains and slavery!

[*He swallows gin. Sirens stop. Slamming of doors. Silence.* Able *puts down glass, advances in crouched*

### ABLE

Wha will be a traitor knave?
Wha can fill a coward's grave?
Wha sae base as be a slave?
Let him turn and flee!
[*speaking*] Welcome, lads!

[*Two* POLICE *wearing vizored helmets appear left in
motorized chairs; another pair to the right. They have
truncheons, handcuffs, lassoes, maybe nets. The next
action must be choreographed by the cast and
director, but at first their efforts to encircle him fail
as he leaps and dodges, crying:*]

### ABLE

Good! . . Well done. . . Yes, nearly! . . Nearly had me
there! . . Oops, another near thing! . . Ouch, yah
you've got me!
[POLICE *entangle him and he goes limp.*]
All right, I surrender, you've definitely got me.
[POLICE *pull the ropes tighter.*]
Ouch – that hurts!
[POLICE *hoist him upside down and handcuff
his ankles together.*]
Hey, there's no need – no need for this!
[*A couple of* POLICE *drag him off by the legs
followed closely by couple pulling out truncheons.
As* ABLE *vanishes off stage he yells in panic:*]
I'm not black! I'm not black!

[*A sharp crack is followed by a sharp scream, another
crack by another scream, a third crack by silence.*]

# 10 : NEWSPAPER OFFICE

CAST : REPORTER a younger, thinner man in a short-sleeved shirt, open necked, EDITOR long-sleeved shirt, bow tie, unbuttoned waistcoat, SUB-EDITOR stouter man in short-sleeved shirt with loosened necktie – all these wear spectacles, MISS SHY as in scene 9, still walking tall.

*The three newspapermen face the audience side by side behind a table long enough to allow plenty of elbow room.* REPORTER *and* SUB *have a screen, keyboard, cordless phone, notepad and pencil, the* EDITOR *only a phone. All seem tired of their jobs. The* EDITOR *leans as far back as possible with closed eyes and hands clasped behind head.* REPORTER *and* SUB *tap their keyboards listlessly with one hand:* SUB *sips from a coffee mug in the other.*

### EDITOR
[*without moving*]
We've a hole on page five. Anything from the police?

### REPORTER
[*taps twice then reads*]
Jobless Hypermaniac Wrecks West End Pub.

[EDITOR *yawns.* SUB *notices.*]

### SUB
I'm bored by jobless hypermaniacs. The whole nation's bored by jobless hypermaniacs.

### EDITOR
[*without moving*]
Try the courts.

                       NEWSPAPER
                       OFFICE

[*puts down mug, taps twice, reads*]
Not much . . . This might raise a laugh . . . In
magistrate court today thirty-three-year-old Able
McMann of no fixed abode, no previous record,
was charged with vandalizing a phone et cetera.
Asked how did he plead he pointed straight at
the magistrate, screamed "Guilty!" and kept
screaming guilty and pointing at magistrate until
dragged out. He's being held for a psychiatric
report. Telephone Vandal Judges Judge?

REPORTER
Not judge. Magistrate.

SUB
Readers don't know the difference.

REPORTER
[*reading screen*]
Able McMann is the hypermaniac who wrecked
Bonham's lounge last night.

EDITOR
[*not moving*]
How?

REPORTER
I don't have that.

SUB
I've got it. [*taps twice, reads*] He maliciously
destroyed public telephone – used menacing
language to the terror of the lieges – ejected barstaff
by physical force – stole excisable liquors and

SUB [*continued*]

challenged the police – resisted arrest with skilful use of boxer-kicks and karate-chops which knocked four policemen out of their chairs before they managed to haul him in. Yes, and a slum landlord has charged him with absconding with a week's rent arrears.

REPORTER
[*impressed*]
They should have rounded it off by planting cocaine on him.

EDITOR
[*opening his eyes*]
He's earned more than half a column. Is his CV on the world-wide web?

[REPORTER's *phone rings. He lifts it and listens.* SUB *starts tapping and reading aloud as he taps.* EDITOR *sits forward, puts elbows on table midway between* REPORTER *and* SUB, *rests chin on clenched fists without looking left or right.*]

SUB
Good school . . . Studied business at Strathclyde . . . Eight years managerial post with Rock Fire Life . . .

REPORTER
[*into phone*]
She sounds insane but put her through anyway.

SUB
[*tapping and reading*]
Six years ago chair accident left him hyperactive.

REPORTER
[*into phone*]
Exactly who are you?

SUB
[*tapping and reading*]
Through jobs aid got managerial desk with National
Equilibrium. Did well, came off hyperactive register.
Government ends jobs aid, end of story. [*Stops tapping
and leans back.*]

REPORTER
[*into phone*]
What message?

EDITOR
[*without moving*]
Wife and kids?

SUB
[*eyes on screen*]
Divorced. No kids.

EDITOR
[*without moving*]
Pity. We could use kids.

SUB
To make a whole page of it?

REPORTER
[*Loudly into phone, waving hand to attract EDITOR.*]
Give me your number quick and I'll phone back.
[*pause*] Got it thanks. Stay there Monica. [*to EDITOR,
putting down handset*] Monica Shy, calling from

REPORTER [*continued*]

payphone. She's McMann's girlfriend, a hypermanic and loony about him. She was also with him in the pub before he tackled the police and she wants us to print his message to the universe. Ready for it?

EDITOR
[*not moving*]
Shoot.

REPORTER

Hypermanics of the world unite! Social inadequates should be proud to go berserk.

EDITOR
[*not moving*]
Call her back and pass her to me.

[*All three lift handsets and clap them to their faces,* REPORTER *after tapping digits.*]

REPORTER
[*into phone*]
Sorry to keep you waiting Monica. Our editor Tom Hume is very interested in your boyfriend's message. Here he is.

EDITOR
[*warm, oily, paternal*]
It's a privilege to speak with you Monica, not many outside phonecalls bring us messages of encouragement and hope. Have you given it to any other papers? [*pause*] Several?

[REPORTER *and* SUB *show alarm, then relief.*]

### EDITOR
*[into phone, unruffled]*
I'm not surprised they weren't interested. Most papers today are too far right for a radical message like that! The Daily Discord is the only British paper to stand up for . . . for . . . to stand up and be counted so we're sending a fast car to fetch you here. *[pause]* No, don't take a taxi, travel at our expense. Where are you? *[pause]* Why the Queen Mother's Maternity Hospital? *[pause]* Who is Betty Macrae?

*[A pause in which* REPORTER *and* SUB *listen intently.]*

### EDITOR
*[into phone, very slowly]*
I . . . seeeee. Yes.

*[*REPORTER *and* SUB *gape at each other in delighted wonder. Still listening hard* EDITOR *points stern finger at* SUB *who swiftly presses digits on his own phone.]*

### EDITOR
*[into phone]*
So Betty Macrae is about to have your boyfriend's baby?

### SUB
*[into phone, fast and quiet]*
Hullo Jock, top priority, lift Monica Shy from Queen Mother's foyer – you'll recognize her, she'll be standing, yes she's a bloody hypermaniac, hurry!

### EDITOR
*[into phone, sharply]*
Twins! When? *[with effort speaks softly]* Early this

EDITOR [*continued*]
morning. What a nice surprise for everyone.
[*musically*] See you soon Monica!

[*All slam handsets down.* REPORTER *and* SUB *laugh,
spin chairs back, career round table in opposite
directions, slapping hands as they pass in front of
it.* EDITOR *resumes his central chin-on-fists pose.*]

EDITOR
[*loudly, without moving*]
Cut the horseplay!

[REPORTER *and* SUB *return to former positions.*]

EDITOR
[*solemnly, without moving*]
This sort of thing restores my faith in God.

SUB
[*reaching for phone*]
Will I tell them to hold the front page?

EDITOR
[*impatient*]
Don't be sodding stupid! This story is a three-day
accumulator so listen hard!

[*He talks with abrupt head and arm movements
watched by* REPORTER *and* SUB *who frequently nod.*]

EDITOR
Day One! Give the page lead on page four to
Hyperactive McMann Runs Amok in West End Pub.
Hyperactive, remember, not Hypermanic or

Hypermaniac, they come later. Play up the rampage.
Interview threatened customers, manhandled
barstaff, stoical police. If the pub interior isn't
damaged show it from outside with stern worried
faces in front and column heads like I was terrifed
and He packs a hefty punch! Get a close-up of the
wrecked telephone.

[*He pauses.* REPORTER *and* SUB *nod.*]

### EDITOR
Then – we're still Day One page five – have his
parents, pals, ex-wife explain why such a decent
respectable citizen went wrong. Get a photograph of
him, even if it shows him as a toddler. Put his head
in the Page One Puff captioned How McMann Went
Wrong exclamation mark but have NOTHING,
NOTHING yet about his sodding bitches and
bastards and message to the nation, right?

### REPORTER and SUB
[*simultaneously*]
Right!

### EDITOR
Day Two! Full page story under four column pic of
Blooming Betty with her Brace of Bastards –

### REPORTER
[*shocked*]
Bairns surely! Bairns!

### EDITOR
Don't interrupt my flow, has the Macrae bitch still
got the hots for the McMann geek?

REPORTER
[*subdued*]
Monica Shy said so.

EDITOR
Great, because on Day Two the Discord is all for
them. We emphasize her sexiness and loyalty –

SUB
[*inspired*]
Eat Your Heart Out, Normals! Blooming Betty
Stands By Her Hypermanic Bonker McMann.

EDITOR
Use a front page splash by Senga Dishart saying
McMann shows the plight of the hyperactive poor
under Humpty Dipsy's welfare cuts. A lot of readers
will like that because most of them are sodding Labour
voters, but Betty's story . . . [*grabs phone, inspired.*]

EDITOR
[*to* REPORTER]
Watch this. You'll learn something. [*into phone*]
Tom Hume. Put me through to someone in charge
of a Queen Mother's post-delivery ward. I don't
know who – they have Betty Macrae, mother of
twins in care. [*to* REPORTER and SUB *who are
watching him, fascinated*] I hope she's got big tits.

REPORTER
Likely at this stage.

EDITOR
Let's give the Tories something too! Frank MacNasty
could mention in his column that he doesn't know

why colleagues are sentimentalizing over a violent
criminal and his slut who . . . [*pause, then into phone: warm, oily, paternal*] Hullo nurse, this is Tom Hume, editor of the Daily Discord. I want to congratulate you and the Queen Mother's for excellent treatment of Betty Macrae and her twa lovely bairns. [*pauses, then chuckles*] Oh, not much escapes us. The Discord is about to start a campaign for natural motherhood. Is Betty breastfeeding her wee weans? [*brief pause*] Good! No danger of milk shortage? [*brief pause*] Good, but that's not my main reason for phoning. [*on intimate note*] Perhaps Betty told you that the father of her twins is in serious trouble? [*brief pause*] No? Never mind. I'm phoning because I have good news for her, news that will take a great weight off her mind. Now, I don't want to intrude, and if she's asleep I'll try some other day but . . . You'll see? Good. [*to* REPORTER and SUB] Big tits in working order. Now to arrange interview and photograph.

SUB
[*pondering*]
Where will we put the picture?

REPORTER
[*sarcastically*]
Put her on page three.

[*With the briefest of delays* EDITOR *and* SUB *give a thumbs-up sign.*]

EDITOR
[*into phone: warm, oily, paternal*]
Hullo Betty, Tom speaking, Tom Hume editor of the

EDITOR [*continued*]

Daily Discord. Monica Shy tells me she recently
gave you a message from your man Able, yes?
[*pause*] Yes and now he's in police custody but I
want you to know that we in the Discord think
society has treated him horribly and we're coming
out strong for him – [*brief pause*]  – yes – [*brief
pause*] – yes but – [*longer pause in which he
grimaces to* REPORTER *and* SUB, *indicating he
endures useless drivel by rotating forefinger against
side of head*] Don't worry, Betty, about money for a
good defence lawyer, leave that with me, I'm
phoning because we're starting to defend him
tomorrow with a strong publicity drive and here's
where we need your help. I know this is a very
hard time for you, a wonderful time but an
exhausting time and I don't want to tire you in
any way at all so this is what I'll do. Hector Brash
and Jenny Aw-Things! Do these names mean
anything to you?  [*brief pause*] He's Scotland's
photographer – photographer royal to the queen –
Jenny's a wonderful reporter and very sympathetic
woman. From nine in the morning to nine at night
I'll have them sitting in the Queen Mother's
waiting-room and if, at any time, you can spare
four or five minutes ask your ward nurse to invite
them in. [*pause, then chuckles*] Of course it will
cost the Discord a lot of money but money doesn't
matter, your happiness and Able's happiness are
what matters . . . [*pause*] You think you can? [*brief
pause*] Bless you Betty! You're a brave good woman.
Bye bye now. [EDITOR *clashes down phone, lies back
in chair with eyes shut, hands clasped behind head
as at first*] Send Brash and Aw-Things straight to
her ward at nine tomorrow.

[*wildly clapping hands*]
Great, Tom! Great! Great!

EDITOR
[*without moving*]
I was wrong about you, Henry.

REPORTER
How, Tom?

EDITOR
You're a good networker but I thought you hadn't
the guts to be a real newsman. I was wrong. [*He
chuckles*.] That notion of an unmarried mother's tits
on the wank page was a stroke of genius! A real
human interest story under the tart pic on the page
three wank page – the Discord will be making
history. The Discord will be setting new standards.

SUB
What if she doesn't look like a sexpot?

EDITOR
Trust Hector Brash! With his angles and lighting
and lab work any bitch with big boobs can be page
three fodder.

REPORTER
[*glumly*]
I meant it as a joke.

EDITOR
[*sits up, grinning*]
The greatest things in the world start as jokes,

EDITOR [*continued*]
laddie! Christianity was a joke before the Romans made it a multinational corporation.

REPORTER
[*sighing*]
What about Day Three? McMann will be out on bail by then.

EDITOR
That's right and by then the big boys will be after him – sleuths from the Moon, the Distress, the Fanfare, the Chimes, the Fender. They can have him. We won't need him then, or Betty Macrae. We'll have the story of Bonker McMann's affair with Monica Shy, first apostle and bearer of his message – [*spreading his arms wide*] – hypermaniacs of the world, unite!

REPORTER
She says he said hypermanics.

EDITOR
Are you sure? Is she sure? Can anyone now be sure of exactly what McMann said in a moment of excitement? The Press Council won't reprimand us for a difference of one letter.

SUB
[*inspired*]
Arch-Hypermaniac Able McMann Calls For Revolution! – all over the front page.

REPORTER
So you're dropping him in the shit?

EDITOR
[*nodding*]
With the biggest splash since the sinking of the Belgrano.

SUB
[*snapping fingers*]
Gotcha!

EDITOR
We'll treat his message as a law-and-order issue. The Discord is on the side of the people against forces of oppression but cannot support a lunatic leftist plotting to overturn society.

REPORTER
Maybe a hyperactive union wouldn't want to overturn society – just help its members.

EDITOR
[*warmly and paternally*]
The Discord's social mission, Henry, is putting excitement into dull lives. Subtle distinctions are for prosperous snobs who read the Chimes or the Fender. Your future is with us. [*pats* REPORTER's *shoulder*] You discovered Able McMann. You gave me Monica Shy. You thought of how to present Betty Macrae. You're going to get a whacking big bonus.

REPORTER
[*humbled and grateful*]
Thanks Tom.

[*Phone rings.* SUB *lifts and listens.*]

SUB
She's at the front desk.

EDITOR
Send her up.

SUB
[*into phone*]
Send her up.

REPORTER
[*sighing*]
I'm sorry for her.

EDITOR
[*sighing*]
Yes, poor Monica. It's a rotten world but we didn't make it. God made it. [*leans back with folded arms*] The best we can do is preserve our honour. We need never feel ashamed if we preserve our honour.

[REPORTER *and* SUB, *stare at him startled.*]

SUB
What is honour, Tom? [*He really wants to know.*]

EDITOR
Doing the job you have chosen as well as you can do it.

[REPORTER *and* SUB *nod solemnly.* EDITOR *suddenly spins his chair back.*]

EDITOR
She's here. Take note.

[EDITOR *rolls to right round the table as* MISS SHY *enters front left, walking as tall as when she left the lounge bar. They meet centre front as* REPORTER *and* SUB *behind them lift pencils, tap keyboards, peer at screens and seem to take notes from them. They only do so when* MISS SHY *speaks.*]

### EDITOR
[*stretching up to shake her hand*]
Welcome Monica! You're as good looking as I expected. No wonder Able fell for you!

### MISS SHY
[*confused*]
He didn't. He doesn't even know my name. I didn't know his until Betty Macrae told me.

### EDITOR
But you like him?

### MISS SHY
I'll love him forever. All my life I've been ashamed of my working legs. He cured me of that. I'll never be ashamed again.

[REPORTER *and* SUB, *scribbling, exchange glances.*]

### EDITOR
[*quickly*]
So now you're shameless, well Able's obviously a man of great charm, immense charisma, the natural leader of a mighty movement. The Discord will pay you – hm – five hundred for exclusive rights to your story of Able and his call for hyperactive unity.

MISS SHY
[*indignant*]
I don't want money!

EDITOR
I know, but think of the help you could give Able at his next court appearance. He's destitute. Will Betty Macrae help him?

MISS SHY
Yes! She loves him too!

EDITOR
[*shaking head*]
You're a cruel girl, Monica. Unless Betty's a very rich woman she'll need all her savings to support Able's weans. And he won't get much help from legal aid nowadays.

[MISS SHY *frowns hard at* EDITOR *for a moment. All wait on her response. It is sudden.*]

MISS SHY
He won't get very much help out of five hundred pounds!

EDITOR
Good for you! How much do you want?

MISS SHY
[*troubled*]
I know so little about these things!

EDITOR
Ten hundred.

## MISS SHY
Perhaps I should consult someone else before committing myself . . .

## EDITOR
Miss Shy, we are the only paper interested in giving the world Able's message! But since it's a hopeful message – and because we admire your guts – we offer twelve hundred for exclusive rights and not a penny more.

## MISS SHY
[*suddenly bold*]
Fifteen hundred!

## EDITOR
Ouch, this hurts! I'll have to take advice! [*to* Reporter *and* Sub] What do you say boys? Should she get fifteen?

## REPORTER and SUB
[*together*]
Yes!

## EDITOR
Outnumbered three to one. Miss Shy, you've beat me. Put it there! [*Shakes hands with her.*]

## MISS SHY
[*astonished*]
This is the first bargain I've ever struck.

## EDITOR
[*suddenly brisk*]
Now, Monica, I feel distinctly hungry. So must you.

EDITOR [*continued*]

We'll discuss details of our campaign over a meal. Working legs go faster than wheels indoors so go down to the front desk, order a car for Tom Hume and wait inside when it comes. I won't be far behind. Off you go!

[MISS SHY *hesitates, puzzled by his abruptness. He smiles at her.*]

### EDITOR
[*very oily and paternal*]
Off! You! Go!

[*She nods and walks briskly out.* REPORTER *looks after her gloomily,* EDITOR *impassively,* SUB *grins.*]

### EDITOR
[*after a pause*]
Poor Monica. She was never taught to think in thousands.

### SUB
Never give a sucker an even break! [*laughs heartily*]

### EDITOR
[*to reporter*]
Shocked are you?

### REPORTER
Less than I'd have been an hour ago. [*He sighs*]

### EDITOR
[*with approval*]
You're learning. Tell Brash and Aw-Things what to

do tomorrow. Have an exclusive rights contract ready for signature when I bring her back. [*to* SUB] Start internetting! Find the right addresses then send Snout, Muzzle, Hatchett and Killiebunkie to interview McMann's parents, pals, ex-wife et cetera. [*rolls offstage saying*] The story of Able McMann and his doxies will be launched, wrapped up and trashed before next week's royal divorce. It's a wonderful thing to be stitching the seamless garment of life's rich tapestry.

[SUB *taps busily on keyboard and without stopping glances sideways at* REPORTER *who slumps at the table, hand supporting head.*]

SUB
What's up? [*Busily tapping*]

REPORTER
[*without moving*]
He's wrong about God.

SUB
Eh? [*frowning but still tapping*]

REPORTER
[*preparing to tap*]
God didn't make this world. We make it.

SUB
[*tapping*]
Maybe, but we can't change it now.

[REPORTER *taps, stares at screen, taps again, stares again then seizes telephone.*]

REPORTER
*[into phone]*

Front desk? MacFarlan of editorials here. The chief is on the way out. Catch him before he leaves and put him on to me. [*to* SUB, *putting down phone*] Able McMann is now at the Western Infirmary. He had a massive heart attack in his police cell two hours ago.

SUB
*[Overjoyed, flinging his arms up]*
Glory, glory, hallelujah!

Ernest Kyle                                    as the Editor

# 11 : SURGICAL THEATRE
## (A SHADOW-PLAY)

CAST : prone, passive ABLE. In gowns and masks, a NURSE, SISTER, ANAESTHETIST, HOUSE OFFICER, SURGEON. Also ADMINISTRATOR, male or female .

*Low back lighting casts silhouettes of* ABLE *prone on low central table, and to one side a structure of cylinders, bottles, tubes, dials, wires with* SISTER *adjusting valve on a suspended bottle. A rubber tube runs from a cylinder to a mask which* ANAESTHETIST *holds over* ABLE's *face. On opposite side* HOUSE OFFICER *sits observing him beside* NURSE *who is arranging instruments on a tray.*

### SOUND
[*Hiss of gas and murmur of conversation*]

[*Enter* SURGEON *who rolls into space behind* ABLE. NURSE *hands* SURGEON *rubber gloves.* SURGEON *pulls them on saying:*]

### SURGEON
So this is Able McMann. The eyes of the media are on us! We must not do less than our usual best. What, Mrs Anaesthetist, is the patient's condition?

### ANAESTHETIST
Steady, Mr McKinnon.

### SURGEON
Colour?

### ANAESTHETIST
Good.

SURGEON
Pulse?

ANAESTHETIST
Regular sinus rhythm.

SURGEON
Blood gases?

HOUSE OFFICER
Normal.

SURGEON
Let's open him up. Scalpel.

[Nurse *hands it. He leans forward and makes one strong steady vertical incision, hands scalpel to nurse and pulls edges of cut open with hands.*]

SOUND
[*Amplified beating of a human heart.*]

SURGEON
Forceps . . . retractor . . . clamp . . . sutures . . . swabs . . .

[Nurse *hands him these. His fingers are busy within the chest.* House Officer *leans over watching closely from the other side.*]

SURGEON
Suction . . .damn!

HOUSE OFFICER
What's the problem?

SOUND
[*Heart rhythm accelerates.*]

ANAESTHETIST
[*consulting dials*]
Blood pressure falling!

SURGEON
Open up the drip. Run in haemocell and FFP.

[SISTER *and* ANAESTHETIST *turn valves.*]

SURGEON
[*muted triumph*]
Aha! A minor haemorrhage. Well . . . maybe not so
minor. [*with sudden urgency.*] Diathermy! Fry those
bleeders!

[NURSE *hands instrument to* HOUSE OFFICER *who
employs it in cavity.*]

SOUND
[*sizzle*]

[HOUSE OFFICER *returns instrument to nurse.*]

SURGEON
[*rapidly*]
Cross-match eight units of packed cells! House
Officer! Insert a long line for rapid access. Large
cannula. Move it!

[*From structure with monitor screen* SISTER *passes a
cable ending in needle to* HOUSE OFFICER, *who inserts it
into vein of patient's neck.*]

SOUND
[*Heartbeat becomes slow and hesitant.*]

SURGEON
[*grumbling*]
More suction sister. Hurry, it's like a swamp in here.

HOUSE SURGEON
What's happening Mr McKinnon? Why has the patient gone off?

SURGEON
[*working busily*]
Unstable myocardium. Or CVA with coning. Or idiosyncratic hypersensitivity reaction – common among hyperactives.

SOUND
[*Loud bleeping from monitors*]

SURGEON
Is that VF?

SISTER
Afraid so.

SURGEON
Right. I'm going to shock him. The de-fibrillator! [*Takes it from* NURSE] Charging . . . Ready . . . Stand clear!

SOUND
[*Loud electric sizzle*]

[ABLE's *body convulses, lies still.*]

SURGEON
[*bending closer*]
No good. He's still fibrillating. IV lignocaine! Stat!

[SISTER *lifts hypodermic syringe and injects it into
the line into neck.*]

SOUND
[*Heart beat stops.*]

SURGEON
Monitor?

HOUSE OFFICER
[*staring at box in structure*]
He's flat-lining.

SURGEON
Dammit, inject intra-cardiac adrenaline!

[NURSE *passes syringe to* HOUSE OFFICER *who leans
forward and injects it into heart.*]

SURGEON
Well? Well?

ANAESTHETIST
Not a blip. We're losing him.

SURGEON
[*grimly*]
Open massage is our only chance, move fast, scalpel,
forceps, retractor, clamp, suture, swabs, anything!

[HOUSE OFFICER *and* SISTER *manipulate things in*

*cavity.* SURGEON's *regular elbow movements show he is squeezing the heart manually.*]

### SOUND
[*Hesitantly the heartbeat starts again.*]

### NURSE
He's coming up!

### SURGEON
More bicarb!

### SOUND
[*Heartbeat becomes slow but firm.*]

### ANAESTHETIST
Sinus rhythm is restored!

[SISTER *turns to consult monitor.*]

### SISTER
Observations stable, respiration spontaneous – you've done it, Mr McKinnon!

[SURGEON *withdraws from table, pulling off mask.*]

### SURGEON
[*wearily, to* HOUSE OFFICER]
Close him up. [*wearily, to* SISTER] Drinks all round.

[*The* SISTER *rolls out.*]

### *ANAESTHETIST*
[*Pulling off mask and clapping hands cheerfully*]
Yes, drinks all round! He's alive! You've saved him!

SURGEON
[*yawning and shrugging wearily*]
More or less.

[*The* HOUSE OFFICER *is stitching up* ABLE *helped by*
NURSE *as* SISTER *returns with tray of glasses and*
*bottle of spirits,* ADMINISTRATOR *close behind.*]

SOUND
[*Heartbeat fades into silence.*]

SISTER
Mr McKinnon, the Senior Administrator wants a
word.

SURGEON
[*incredulous*]
You! Why are you here? Administrators bugger off
home at half past four.

SENIOR ADMINISTRATOR
[*unperturbed*]
I'm interested in this case because –

SURGEON
[*stripping off gloves*]
Next of kin, are you?

ADMINISTRATOR
[*patiently*]
– because the Secretary of State is interested in this
case.

SURGEON
Wants to chuck him back in jail does he?

ADMINISTRATOR
[*impatient*]
Of course not – this is a clear case for clemency. The health service will be highly embarrassed if this particular chap dies on us because a lot of wets claim he's a martyr to some sort of social breakdown. Will he die on us?

[Sister *has filled glasses.* Surgeon *lifts and contemplates one.*]

SURGEON
Not at once. The operation failed but the patient survived.

ADMINISTRATOR
[*testily*]
What does that mean?

SURGEON
The heart stopped long enough to starve the brain of oxygen. He is in a coma which could last days, weeks, years – or until someone turns off his drip-feed. Your health! [*He raises the glass.*]

ADMINISTRATOR
The Secretary of State won't like that at all. Our private investors won't like it much either. Is there nothing you can do?

SURGEON
Yes, I can drink their healths. Health to all of us!
[*He drinks.*]

# 12 : HOSPITAL WARD

CAST : ABLE, DOCTOR, BETTY, MANAGER, EDITOR, MISS SHY and OTHER AVAILABLE MEMBERS OF CAST.

*Darkness with the slow, steady ticking of a clock. After half a minute the Westminster chimes sound the three quarter hour. There is a moment of silence than a very brief flash of light shows most of the cast standing round a bed.*

### BETTY'S VOICE
[*in darkness*]
He blinked! He blinked!

### SOMEONE ELSE'S VOICE
[*in darkness*]
His eyes are still shut.

### DOCTOR'S VOICE
[*in darkness*]
There was definite eye movement. There is definite eye movement!

*Light comes on.* ABLE *blinks at audience from his hospital bed, centre stage. He wears hospital gown, is propped up on pillows, with drip feed into bandaged right arm from suspended bottle.* DOCTOR *stands on drip feed side with fingers on* ABLE's *pulse.* BETTY *sits on other side with her hand on* ABLE's *other hand. Gathered round is everyone else in the play except* MISS SHY. *The* MANAGER *is close to* BETTY's *side.* EDITOR, *with notebook and pen, is on edge of group on* DOCTOR's *side, scribbling from time to time.* ABLE *looks from side to side then his gaze fixes on* BETTY. *He opens his mouth, tries to speak, fails to speak, licks his lips and tries again.*

### ABLE
[*slowly and feebly*]
Hull . . . hullo Betty.

### BETTY
Oh Able! [*She weeps with joy.*]

### ABLE
[*puzzled*]
This . . . this isn't prison is it? Why . . . why are all these people here? [*feebly gestures to them*]

### BETTY
They're all friends and you're in a proper hospital and you'll never go to prison again!

### ABLE
[*still confused*]
Why . . . how long was I asleep?

### BETTY
[*weeping*]
A long time! A long time!

### DOCTOR
[*briskly*]
You have been in coma for seven months and sixteen days. I'm glad you've come out of it, we need this bed for someone else.

[DOCTOR *detaches drip feed, swabs* ABLE'S *arm and*

### ABLE
[*shaking head*]
Seven months  . . . don't cry Betty . . . Eye Tee, why are you here?

### MANAGER
To tell you that a desk in quality control is yours whenever you return to us. National Equilibrium is a company which cares.

### EDITOR
[*making note*]
The Daily Discord will tell it to the universe.

### MANAGER
Thanks!

### EDITOR
And you have no money worries, Able. The Daily Discord has a small fortune in a bank account for you.

### ABLE
[*perplexed*]
The Daily Discord . . .

### EDITOR
[*chuckling*]
The British press is as sentimental as the British public. After your stroke we started a sympathy fund to give you the best healthcare money could buy. You've more than fourteen thousand left.

*Scene Twelve* Enough downpayment for a mortgage on a bungalow in Milngavie!

ABLE
[*radiantly happy*]
With later, perhaps, a holiday home in Arran!

DOCTOR
[*warningly*]
Less general excitement please. Stand back, I have tests to make.

[*All but the* DOCTOR *withdraw a little,* BETTY *waving to* ABLE *reassuringly.*]

DOCTOR
[*to* ABLE]
Raise your right arm.

[ABLE *slowly does so.*]

DOCTOR
Move it from side to side.

[ABLE *slowly does so.*]

DOCTOR
Drop it . . . [*feels* ABLE's *pulse*] . . . Now try the left.

[ABLE *lifts and moves the left arm.*]

DOCTOR
Good. Drop it. Are you able to sit up?
[*stands back slightly.*]

[ABLE, *pushing with his arms, sits clear of the*
*supporting pillows.* BETTY *gasps with delight, others*
*murmur approval.* DOCTOR *flings clothes aside*
*exposing* ABLE's *legs.*]

### DOCTOR
Can you get your feet to the floor?

[*With great effort* ABLE *gets feet to floor and sits on*
*bed edge, gasping for breath.* DOCTOR *leans forward,*
*lifts* ABLE's *right leg and supports it on his lap.*]

### DOCTOR
[*holding* ABLE's *toes*]
Wiggle your toes.

### ABLE
[*strains*]

### DOCTOR
[*holding* ABLE's *ankle*]
Flex your ankle.

### ABLE
[*strains*]

### DOCTOR
[*gripping calf*]
Can you raise your knee?

### ABLE
[*straining*]
No!

[DOCTOR *solemnly lowers Able's foot to the floor.*

ABLE *and everyone else stare at* DOCTOR, *hopefully.*]

## DOCTOR
[*solemnly*]

It's perhaps rather early to say so but I believe he is almost completely paralysed from the waist down.

## EVERYONE
Hooray!

[*While others shake hands, slap each other's shoulders, laugh, or grin,* EDITOR *grins and scribbles,* ABLE *shakes his head in wondering astonishment at his good luck,* BETTY *rolls round the bed to him. Only* DOCTOR *stays impassive.*]

## DOCTOR
[*loudly, clapping hands*]
Chair!

[*A wheelchair more excitingly modern than any we have seen is pushed so forcefully on stage that it stops near the bed.* DOCTOR *and* BETTY *help* ABLE *into it.*]

## ABLE
[*wondering*]

When I remember all that's happened to me. . . when I remember the years between my road accident and waking up just now . . . they seem, apart from meeting you Betty dear . . . [*squeezes her hand*] . . . they seem a nightmare. An impossible nightmare!

## BETTY
But you're awake at last and THIS is real!

[*She embraces him. Widespread emotion.* EDITOR *pockets notebook, advances to front stage and addresses audience.* ABLE *and* BETTY *continue embracing. The rest of the company politely turn their backs on them and attend to* EDITOR, *standing to left and right of him.*]

### EDITOR

Ladies and gentlemen, you may have noticed that this play has no hero. Able McMann is just an ordinary man who started life a bit luckier than most folk and by sheer accident got worse for a while. But though we have no hero you perhaps think me a bit of a villain –

### ANYONE ELSE
Surely Humpty Dipsy is the villain!

### EDITOR

Nonsense. Prime ministers haven't the strength to be villains. They just do what stock exchanges let them. No, I am the one consciously selfish guy in this play and I'm proud of it. Our happy ending was made posible by me – me and the Daily Discord.

### MISS SHY
[*yelling offstage*]
No! No! No! No!

[MISS SHY, *walking tall, strides on with placard saying HYPERMANICS OF THE WORLD UNITE! She glares from the company to the audience.*]

### MISS SHY
[*loudly*]
This is NOT a happy ending! It is NOT! It is NOT!

Patsy Morrison
as
Miss Shy

[*Apart from* ABLE *and* BETTY *who continue embracing as if nothing had occurred the rest express annoyance, impatience or amusement.* EDITOR *winks at audience, rotating forefinger against side of his head.*]

# THE END

*THIS MAY BE SIGNALLED BY LIGHTS GOING OUT, THEN FULL LIGHTING IS RESTORED TO SHOW THE CAST, WITH ALL WHO ARE ABLE TO STAND BOWING TO THE AUDIENCE. ANOTHER ENDING COULD BE:*

EDITOR
[*to audience*]
Happy or not, this is definitely . . .

THE WHOLE CAST
[*in unison*]
**The! End!**

# PRODUCTION NOTES

DESPITE HAVING A CAST list of thirty-eight characters this play could be acted by an energetic company of fifteen or an unusually energetic company of twelve.

A perfect production would have all wheelbound characters played by wheelbound actors, thus saving rent of chairs. Those acting the Social Worker and Benefits Tribunal would also be blind and deaf. Perfection is not always possible, but sighted actors can play convincingly blind by wearing opaque glasses padded to stop them seeing. The four actors playing the Benefit Tribunal should learn sign-language from someone fluent at it as most audiences will notice if actors are inventing meaningless gestures and some signs (the one for "Get rid of him" for instance) can be read by anyone. A production in which the Tribunal's sign-speech appears as words on a screen will gain in humour but lose in sinister effect.

A few words and phrases show that this is a Scottish play, but companies from other places can change these into idioms of their own province. When preparing to fight the police Able could sing *The Wearing of the Green, Men of Harlech, Ilkley Moor Ba' T'at* or *Land of Hope and Glory* instead of *Scots Wha Hae*. But nearly all characters are middle class so most English speaking companies may be smart enough to act the whole play without changing it.

Companies lacking resources to act the shadow play may substitute the following for Scene 11.

# ALTERNATIVE SCENE 11

CAST: POLITICIAN and HIGH COURT JUDGE.
The POLITICIAN sits gloomily nursing a balloon of brandy. JUDGE enters with similar glass, smiling. His presence is acknowledged with a dreary nod.

JUDGE
[*playfully*]
Does something depress us?

POLITICIAN
[*gloomily*]
It does.

JUDGE
Are the initials Ay Em?

POLITICIAN
Yes. Excitement about the Able McMann case is mounting at the wrong time for us. The public were bored by the plight of the hyperactive poor until the damned Daily Discord made it interesting again.

JUDGE
[*slyly teasing him*]
The Chimes says nationwide interest in McMann has nothing to do with his disease – it merely shows a widespread middle-class dread of unemployment and failing pension funds.

POLITICIAN
[*grimly nodding*]
Quite so. It's an issue that might force a change of Government.

JUDGE
[*chuckling*]
Nonsense! The middle class knows which side its bread is buttered. It'll never restore anything you destroy.

POLITICIAN
In this case it may. In this case we may – just for a while. I told the press that McMann was only destitute because he hadn't explored all available benefit channels. This has caused such a spate of enquiries that Social Welfare is under pressure to restore some former benefits. Did you see McMann's women on Cosmorama last night?

JUDGE
[*nodding*]
The Shy hypermanic was obviously deranged but his former social worker and the mother of his children spoke well.

POLITICIAN
[*sighing*]
We can no longer dismiss his supporters as loony leftists. Eye Tee of National Equilibrium has spoken out for him.

JUDGE
[*puzzled*]
Why does the head of a respectable British company resort to such cynically exploitational advertising?

POLITICIAN
National Equilibrium needs a caring image to distract from its child labourers in the Caribbean.

Indeed? I have shares in that company. Any news *Cosy*
from the hospital?                                *Club*

### POLITICIAN
None. He's still in coma. They don't know when or if
he'll emerge from it. He could stay that way for weeks,
months, years before they pull the plug on him.

### JUDGE
Might that not happen sooner rather than later?
Accidentally, I mean?

### POLITICIAN
A stupid idea. He must not be made a martyr. That's
how movements start.

### JUDGE
[*emphatically*]
No movement!

### POLITICIAN
Nip it in the bud!

### JUDGE
Return Able McMann to decent obscurity by the
shortest possible route. We won't prosecute.

### POLITICIAN
[*wearily*]
Yes an obvious case for clemency. God damn him
let's order lunch.

# HOW
# THIS PLAY GOT WRITTEN

**B**IRDS OF PARADISE is a professional theatre company providing professional drama training for people with physical disabilities. It also tours with professional productions. Formed in 1989, in 1993 it became a limited company and a registered charity, taking a new name from Ronald Laing's book *Sweet Bird of Paradise* which it had partly dramatized. When I was asked to write a play for it in 1996 the Council of Management was as follows:

**Forrest Alexander**, wheelchairbound by multiple sclerosis.

**Iain Carmichael**, chairman, car salesman with experience of theatre company management.

**Andrew Dawson**, art director and fully qualified drama therapist.

**David Maclean**, director at the Alpha Project resource centre for people with disabilities.

**Patsy Morrison**, administrator.

**Sylvia Sandeman**, paraplegic, disability consultant with Spinal Injuries Scotland.

At that time only only Mr Dawson and Ms Morrison were salaried.

The suggestion that I write a play for the company came from Forrest Alexander. He knew me as a novelist and thought that, since novels and plays equally depend on characters, dialogue and settings, any saleable novelist could write a successful play. This is not always true, as Henry James discovered on the first night of his play *Guy Domville*. Had I only written prose fiction I would have rejected Forrest's suggestion. However, in the days of a long-forgotten Labour administration I had seven radio, eleven television, four stage plays networked or performed, and was a highly inefficient minutes secretary of *The Scottish Society of Playwrights*, a small trade union started by CP Taylor and Tom Gallagher. My career as professional dramatist ended in 1978 with the death of Francis Head, my London agent, but I still felt able to write plays so Forrest introduced me to the company.

From the 6th of June to the 22nd of August I had nine meetings with actors and friends of the company, always at 5 pm on Thursdays, always with Andrew Dawson or Patsy Morrison present, and all but once at the company office near Glasgow Cross, in a large room where we sat round a table among the vivid creations of a disabled folks' art class.

To the first meeting I brought only one idea. The play must have strong parts for as many disabled actors as possible, so should be set in a world where the able-bodied were a pitiable minority. The company thought this amusing. Forrest Alexander suggested a wheelchair benefit tribunal to which the able-bodied would (unsuccessfully) appeal. Mrs Anne Marie Robertson suggested that the tribunal might be a dumb one which spoke to the appellants through an artificial voice box. This grotesque notion was along lines I wanted, but I needed to know the

everyday embarrassments of being disabled so that
my able-bodied hero could suffer these also. I was
told how hard it is for people in wheelchairs to get
service in pubs if not accompanied by an able-bodied
friend. Mrs Robertson, who has been wheelchairbound for many years, spoke of some normal people's
inability to accept that she was married with three
children. When asked, "How did you manage that?"
she had to smile and shrug her shoulders. She once
had to refuse a good job because acceptance meant
flitting to a house where light-switches, taps, cooker
and other essential things were out of her reach and
there was no money to re-equip it.

At this first meeting I also heard that my idea
was not original. Vic Finkelstein, senior lecturer in
disability studies at the Open University, had set a
story in a village designed for the badly disabled.
The able-bodied who cared for them were
endangered by low doors, ceilings and wheeltracks
linking the buildings. Central Television had issued
a video cartoon of this story. It makes the same social
point as Working Legs while being more informative
about needs of disabled folk, but differs in plot and
characters. I have consciously stolen from Mr
Finkelstein the low door in scene 2 and Able's offer
to wear a safety helmet.

A week later I met Alistair Fleming, a student of
architecture before being hit by a car. It had left him
partly paralysed and had damaged his short-term
memory. He knew my novel Lanark because he had
read it before the accident and he told me his own
story in a jocular way, saying he had been very lucky
– in his parents. When hospital treatment stopped

doing him good his mother gave up her job to nurse him at home, and both parents had used their savings to fight a long legal battle with the car's insurance company. They won. Alistair now lives in a house adapted to his needs and employs a truly Christian minder. At a third meeting I met Mrs Alice Thompson who suggested her own medical experience could give my play a happy ending. A married woman and working nurse, she had undergone an operation for a heart condition and suffered a stroke during it. She recovered consciousness seven months later without the use of her legs.

This gallant willingness to make fun of terrible experience made my job easy. I wrote the first two scenes in time for the fourth meeting. From then on we sat round the table reading scenes aloud as they were added and discussing how the play should go. Ernest Kyle, who suffers from emphysema and is also a writer, suggested that Able's legginess should have led to the breakdown of an earlier marriage. Ernest invented the concept of wheel-training, wrote the tender dialogue which ends scene 4 and gave detailed information upon how our government is deliberately breaking down the social welfare services. As we read on it grew easy to see readers in particular parts. John Campbell seemed right for Able McMann because prosthetic surgery in both legs lets him walk with a completely natural appearance, yet his thoughtful, anxious face indicates life is not easy. Anne Marie seemed suited to the manager or Meg. It was she who suggested Able's ankles be handcuffed.

The Birds of Paradise Company has received

generous grants from Glasgow City and Scottish Arts Councils whose logos are these:

This has helped the company to enlarge its staff and engage with forty-five drama workshops throughout Scotland. The number is growing. These cater for a wide range of disabilities while containing many people without them. At present most of them are rehearsing *Working Legs*; but the parent company has commissioned a new play from the author Archie Hind which will go into rehearsal when *Working Legs* goes on tour in 1998.

The grants have also helped us publish this book in time for Christmas 1997. Plays are usually published after the first stage production, but the condition of Scottish theatre makes the reverse order just as sensible.

It remains for me to thank Christopher Boyce for advice on how to make scene 10 more convincing, and for suggesting the reappearance of Miss Shy at the end; also Angela Mullane for help with legal details; also Doctors Bruce Charleton and Gillian Rye for dialogue in the surgical operation scene; also Scott Pearson and Joe Murray who between them typed and typeset this book under the author's hideously exacting regime.

*Alasdair Gray*
*Glasgow 14-11-1997*